Coaching The Home Team

Coaching the

HOME TEAM

Winning the game of parenting and getting the most out of your child

JASON TAYLOR

NEW YORK

LONDON • NASHVILLE • MELBOURNE • VANCOUVER

Coaching The Home Team

Winning the game of parenting and getting the most out of your child

© 2018 Jason Taylor

Published in New York, New York, by Morgan James Publishing. Morgan James is a trademark of Morgan James, LLC. www.MorganJamesPublishing.com

The Morgan James Speakers Group can bring authors to your live event. For more information or to book an event visit The Morgan James Speakers Group at www.TheMorganJamesSpeakersGroup.com.

ISBN 9781683505020 paperback
ISBN 9781683505037 eBook
Library of Congress Control Number: 2017904095

Cover and Interior Design by:
Chris Treccani
www.3dogcreative.net

In an effort to support local communities, raise awareness and funds, Morgan James Publishing donates a percentage of all book sales for the life of each book to Habitat for Humanity Peninsula and Greater Williamsburg.

Get involved today! Visit
www.MorganJamesBuilds.com

CONTENTS

INTRODUCTION

I was born into a family of nine kids and to loving parents who would do anything to take care of us with all of the love and guidance they possessed. We had a small home in Aurora, Colorado, and I lived there until I moved out of the house after I graduated from W. C. Hinkley High School in Aurora.

One of the very first pictures of me that I have was of me as a small child holding a softball in my hand. In the picture, the softball looks as though it was bigger than my head. My older sister Pam was an athlete, and she is the one who taught me to play baseball and really got me excited about the sport. I have been playing ever since. I was usually the smallest guy on the team growing up, and I when I started, like most young athletes, I played whatever position my coach needed me to play.

I always had a really strong arm, so one day my coach asked me to pitch, so I did. I really enjoyed it and was getting a little frustrated because I would strike the batter out and the catcher would miss the ball, thus allowing the batter to get to first base. I told my coach that I wanted to catch, and that was the beginning of a lifetime behind the plate.

I have been playing baseball in that position since that day. I occasionally fill in at other positions, but the majority of my entire career to this day has been behind the plate. I have always seen myself as the captain of the team, a natural leader, and I believe that the captain usually resides behind home plate.

As the captain, I made sure that I knew what every position's responsibility was on the field and then was able to call out commands as plays were taking place on the field and put my teammates in a position to make a play.

Through the years, the other athletes around me grew, and I did not. It seemed like I was always the small skinny kid on the team, and because of this I always felt that I had to work a little harder and perform a little better in order to keep up with the stronger, bigger, faster athletes on my team. At the time, I thought this was a curse, and now, looking back on it, I believe it to have been a blessing. Having to work hard and prove myself on the field over and over again has made me into the person I am today.

The other athletes really started to get bigger than I was when I entered high school, and from the first day of high school tryouts, I really felt judged by my size and looks and not my ability. For the first time in my baseball life, I was put with the kids who couldn't play as well. In fact, the first person I was playing catch with missed one of my throws during warmups and it smacked him right in the nose. He ended up going to the trainers' office just after practice had begun. My first thoughts were, *Oh, no, is this what high school is going to be like?* Fortunately for me, my second thought was, *I will do anything to move from this group to the starters.*

For the next four years, I spent my evenings and weekends playing baseball, and when I wasn't at school practicing, I was at home throwing at the side of the garage or hitting off the tee. This brings me to another point: Growing up in such a big family, my mom was a stay-at-home mom, and my dad owned his own company. We always had enough, but we never seemed to have any extra. If I wanted something for baseball, I had to earn it. So I learned very young to offer myself for weed pulling or mowing my mom's friends' yards for the baseball equipment or fees I needed in order to play.

Often I would do work for my older brother Kevin, who has always been eager to help me out. I also helped my brothers on a paper route that my mom signed us up for, and she would drive us around in her red Subaru wagon while we delivered the morning paper to the homes in the neighborhood across the creek from our house. At the time, I thought this was a curse because I had to get up so early and work so hard at what I thought was such a young age, and in hindsight, I could not be more grateful for the experience that growing up in my family has given me. It has shaped me into the person I am, and it has given me the opportunity to clarify what I want to get out of my life.

Throughout my life, I have played for a number of coaches, from the dads who were just there to fill in and help out, to the lifetime coaches who had their set ways of doing things, most of whom were not open to new ideas. Some coaches I had a lot of fun playing for, and others I did not appreciate at all. But I was equally happy to move on to the next level team as well.

You see, if I was on a baseball field, I was having fun and it has always been that way for me. Although I played on a lot of winning teams, and we experienced a lot of success, it wasn't until I walked on at Mesa Community College in Arizona that I first experienced a real coach. I say this with the upmost respect for all the coaches I had before that day, and I love them for what they taught me. It's just that there was clearly something different about this coach.

The story of how I came to play for Mesa was an interesting twist of fate and a funny one, so I want to share it with you because it will explain a lot.

At first I wasn't even going to go to college; I was just going to continue working like I had been doing since I was fourteen. Then I met my wife—no, I didn't know it at the time—but she was the most amazing woman I had ever met, and it took me weeks of working with her to even talk to her. She is amazing!

She was still a senior in high school and I had just graduated, so I was a little older than she was. When we started dating, she had already committed to the University of Northern Colorado where she was going to be studying to be a teacher. I had no interest in being a teacher and really had no interest in college, but I wanted to be close to her so I enrolled and got accepted to the same university and was all set to go to school in the fall.

I tried out for the team, and made the club baseball team. This was the first time in my life where no amount of work, effort, or commitment on my part seamed to make a difference to the head coach. I finally asked the coach what it would take for me to catch for the varsity team. I felt as though I was better at the position than his starter and I was a better hitter, but still I felt that I was not even given a chance to compete for the position.

The answer my coach gave me blew my mind, and bears repeating word for word here: "You are too small—in order to catch at this level you would have to gain about seventy pounds." I still think that he was actually joking when he said that, as I sensed a sort of mocking tone when he was saying it. My first thought was not what you might think; it was not a thought of disappointment, but a thought of hope. I now had what I needed, a new goal. I was going to gain seventy pounds.

For the first time in my life, I committed to building bulk. I went to the team trainer and between the two of us, we came up with a meal plan and a workout plan that was incredibly intense and would require a lot of commitment on my part. In fact, the trainer thought that I should start slower and work my way into it, but I told him no way, I was all in and needed to get this done so that I could catch for the varsity team.

The new workout plan required me to hit the gym twice a day, to reduce my running and increase my strength training, and I ate six meals a day and took Creatine before every workout. Over the next two months, I grew from five feet eight inches tall to six feet even. I gained seventy-seven pounds of almost pure muscle.

When I went back to coach to compete for my position at catcher now that I had done exactly what he said I needed to do, he had already assigned me to the club team for the spring season and the job was already taken.

I was devastated. I had done exactly what I had been told I needed to do in order for me to have the chance to compete for the varsity spot, and yet here I was being told by the same person that I was not going to get the chance to compete even though I was now the "right size" to be a catcher at this level.

So I started looking around at other colleges in the area, and it seemed too late to change so I agreed, with myself, to make the most of my time with the club team. I ended up making some good friends on the team, and we did have a lot of fun. My girlfriend knew that I was still unhappy being on the club team and not varsity, so she suggested that we take off for spring break.

Somehow we decided to go to Arizona, and I don't exactly remember how it came about, but we scheduled a walk-on tryout for me and one of my friends, who was traveling with us, at Mesa Community College. The trip ended up being a total fiasco and included our car breaking down, my nearly beating my friend on the side of the road, and getting food poisoning the night before the tryout. I called the coach the day of the tryout and said that I could not make the tryout in the condition I was in, and we agreed to reschedule it.

Later that year, my dad and I went back down to Mesa and I had a private tryout with the coach. It was not a formal tryout like before, just myself and one other player were at the field at that time. This is when I first realized that he was a different kind of coach. After the tryout, which I might add was probably the best tryout I have ever had in my life, he came to me and asked how I thought I had done. I thought for a moment and wanted to say that I had kicked butt and there was no one better for his team than me, but something stopped me, and I simply said, "I could have done better."

He smiled as though that was the exact answer he was looking for, and he then began to tell me that he could not offer me any scholarships because I was out of state, but that he would love to have me as a part of his team. I made the decision right then and there that I wanted to play for him, and I spent the next three years with him in Mesa, Arizona.

There were two things that made him so successful and such a great coach. He believed in me, and he had surrounded himself with a team of coaches that were all better than him at what they did. They were all specialists and knew their role better than anyone else on the field, and he was constantly talking them up and making sure that they knew how much he appreciated them.

I didn't realize it at the time, but he was doing everything he needed to do in order to be the best at what he did. He surrounded himself with a great team and then attracted the best players to his program with that team, and then he proceeded to win, and to win a lot with all the teams he ever put on the field. He also had a real talent for putting his players in a position to succeed. He did the same thing with the coaching staff that he put together.

Playing for him made me realize that I wanted to coach. I didn't know how or what or why, but something inside of me starting burning and I just knew that I was going to be a coach. Thus began my coaching career that continues to this day.

When I left Mesa to go home and marry my wife, I immediately began coaching at my high school and have since coached numerous high school, adult, and youth baseball, basketball, softball, and soccer teams. I have discovered that the one thing I love more than playing baseball is coaching young athletes on how to be successful in their sport, and more importantly, in their lives.

Introduction Review

I tell you my story, not because I want you to know who I am or for validation. I tell my story because you might be thinking to yourself things like, "Well he is different!" or "He doesn't know what I have been through!" or "He doesn't know what I am going through right now!" or "What gives him the right to tell me how to be a better parent and coach?" I just want you to realize that I am a lot like you, and when I started coaching and parenting, I only wish someone had written this book and made it available for me to read. So take what you can from my story and relate it to yours. You will see, we may not be as different as you think.

CHAPTER 1

Who Do You Listen To?

———

I put this chapter right here because I am about to give you my opinion, and you may think because I wrote a book, that makes me qualified to give you my opinion. I would advise you otherwise. Everybody has an opinion, and how much their opinion is worth depends on what you do with it. I want you to read this book with an open heart, an open mind, and at the same time I want you to use discernment in reading this book.

Not everything I say, or every exercise I offer to you through this book is going to resonate with you, and that is okay. I am not here to convince you of my way of thinking or of my way of doing things. I just want to share what I know to be true with you, and from there I expect you to do with it what you will. I want you to take what you can from reading this book and even if you only take one idea, and that one idea changes the way you think just a little, then my intention will be fulfilled in the writing of this book.

One of my mentors on my journey taught me that everyone has opinions, and most people mean well, but not everyone is qualified to give you their opinion. What he meant by this is simply stated: "Take advice, counsel, and opinions from people who have what you want and have been where you are." This is why in the introduction I shared my story with you. If somewhere in the reading of my story you find that I am qualified to give you advice, then keep reading and take what you can from what I am writing for you.

Being an athlete my whole life I have seen a lot, and it still boggles my mind when I am in the gym and I see someone, who is overweight and out of shape, training someone else on how to get into shape! This blows my mind, and then I realize that not only is that person taking their advice, they are also paying them for that advice. That's like saying, "I want to be a professional chef," and then asking someone off the street who has never cooked before to teach you how to be a professional chef. It just doesn't make any sense.

If you are trying to get into shape, doesn't it make sense that you would ask someone who is in shape how to get into shape? If I wanted to be a professional race car driver, I would not go to the teenager who just passed his driver's test and ask him to teach me how to be a professional driver. That just doesn't make sense, yet people take advice blindly all the time from anyone on the street.

I can't tell you how many times my broke friends lectured me how what I was doing at the time was not going to work. They would even offer the reasons why it would not work, even though the person who was mentoring me was currently making millions of dollars doing exactly what I was learning to do. Who are you going to listen to?

Now since this is a book on parenting, I should probably tell you that I am a parent of three of the most incredible young girls, and at the time of the writing of this book they are twelve, ten, and seven years old. And they have taught me everything I know about being a parent. They have taught me what works and what doesn't work. They have taught me what inspires them to achieve more and do more, and what stops them dead in their tracks.

This is what I am going to share with you throughout this book. The principles of success are written in the words and deeds of all our youth. Before someone comes and tells them that they can't do something, they can do it. They have no doubt, no limitations, and all the ability in the world to do anything they want, right up until that moment when someone in a position of authority (usually a parent) tells them that they can't do it.

It absolutely breaks my heart whenever I witness a parent, the person who loves you more than anyone else in the world unconditionally, step on their child's dream and squash it before it has a chance to blossom and grow. Words that are almost never spoken in my home in this order are, "You can't do that." I have come to realize over the years that this simple phrase has killed more dreams than any other phrase, in any language, anywhere on the planet. I will talk about this in a later chapter, but I felt that this was an appropriate time to share a little bit on this subject with you.

Let's get back to the subject of this chapter, who do you listen to? Now that you know that I have something you want, let's talk about the second part of this equation—someone who has been where you are. What does this mean, and why do I care if someone has been where I am? Let's use an example here to simplify this.

Let's say that you want to start your own company, and you are starting with no money and no idea of how to start a company. You just know that you have a great idea, and you want to start your own company in order to get your idea to the market and make a difference. Do you think it would be more powerful and effective to talk with someone who started in the exact same position that you are in right now, or someone who inherited the family company and was born with a silver spoon in his mouth?

Which one of these two examples will know how you feel right now and will have had the same obstacles to overcome that you currently have? Which one do you think will prove more effective in helping you get through any challenges you might face along the way? Why?

It seems obvious, right? Looking at this, you are probably thinking, Well, the guy who has done what I am trying to do and started from the same position I'm in probably is going to give me the best advice, correct? Of course he is.

I will give you a real example from my life. I was approached by a multi-level marketer who had a really compelling pitch. When I did the research on the company, I knew that it was a good company with strong leadership and a great compensation plan. I asked him what level of success he had in the business, and his answer was less than inspiring.

At first, he got defensive as if my questions were an attack on him personally, so I told him why I was asking the question and that it was not a personal attack. I then told him that my best chance of succeeding would be if I could be trained by someone who has what I want and who started where I would be starting in the company.

Eventually, he agreed with me that it would be in both our best interests for me to be trained by someone who was making the kind of money in this business that we wanted to make. Once I spoke to the person who had that information, and she agreed to mentor me, I joined the company. You see, success is not new. Everything you are trying to do has been done before, so why not talk to someone who knows the path? If I wanted to get to San Francisco from Denver and I did not have GPS or a map, who would I ask for directions? Would I ask someone who has never traveled outside of Colorado, or would it make more sense to ask someone who has been to San Francisco?

I know it seems obvious and that I am hammering this point on you right now and this is all true. The reason I am doing this and trying to get you to really understand this, is because this is where it all starts. If you start your journey to success by listening to someone who is a failure, then you are about 90 percent more likely to fail than if you are listening to someone who has the level of success you are trying to achieve.

I know what you are thinking right now: I would never do that, I would never take advice from a failure when I am working on my own success. So let me share a story from my own life, and I want you to listen carefully and see if you have had this conversation before.

At the time of writing this book, I have been working on a big project for almost five years, and the project has been moving forward for the most part. But during that time there have been some setbacks, some more serious than others, and some bigger than others, and my team and I are working diligently right now to make sure this project gets completed. That being said, every time I go to a family gathering, whether it is on my side of the family or my wife's side of the family, it does not matter. The first question I get asked, after the usual "How are you?" is, "Are you still working on that project?" or even worse, "When are you going to give up on that and face reality and get a job so you can support your family?".

In fact, about two years ago I did give up, not on the project of course, but on talking about it around my family. My kids, my wife, and I almost never discuss my project around our family. They all care about my family and me, so they want to give me their two cents, which of course they believe is worth a lot more than that because they know best. I don't say this to them, but in the context of this chapter let's discuss this a little.

Would you listen to someone who has a job they hate, works only to get paid, and has never built a project at all, let alone a development of the size and scope I am working on? Or would you listen to the developer on your team who has done projects like this and knows of others who have done something similar and who says that we can get it done, it's just a matter of time and money?

Everyone knows what I am telling you here, or most people do anyway, and this is probably not the first time you are hearing this. Yet you know there have been times when you were with your friends or family and someone totally unqualified to do so offered you the same or similar advice—to give up on your project and do something different—when you shared your idea with him or her.

My mentor for years has repeatedly told me that "leaders are always readers, and readers always become leaders" and yet, almost every time I am with my family and I am taking a moment to read some new book or reread a book I have read before, someone is constantly giving me a hard time about it and suggesting that I am wasting my time.

I am guessing that since you are reading this book, you are not one of those people and you would not take this kind of unsolicited advice, but let me be really clear: I see this all the time when I am coaching on the field and especially when I am consulting a business owner. Let me repeat, I see people fall victim to this all the time.

Make sure that the person you are listening to has what you want and has been where you are. If not, stay as far away from them as you can, or talk about something other than your success or your business so that they don't have the opportunity to crush your hopes.

Have you noticed the words I am using when I am talking about who you should listen to? I am using words like advice, counsel, suggestions, and I do that on purpose. The final piece on this subject and to close this chapter, let's take this to the next level.

The reason I suggest that you take advice and not take commands is that you are unique. You are you, and that is the one thing no one else is. Think of this world as a puzzle, and it is not complete without your piece, and you will never be complete without the rest of the pieces. That being said, you are the only person on this planet who sees things from your perspective. Not one other person has your exact same experience and filters. You see things differently, and that is what makes you so perfect.

This is where discernment comes into play. You take advice from people who are qualified to give it, then you think about that advice, and you take from it what you can use. Ultimately, you listen to your number one advisor and the one who has always been the closest to you, the one who has been with you your entire life and has gone through every experience you have gone through—and that person is YOU! I am all about getting as much information as possible on whatever subject you are studying, but in the end it is your life and you are the one who has to live with it.

You have to make your own decisions; no one can make them for you, and if you allow them to try, you will not be happy with the outcome. I would suggest that you take what you learn, see how it applies to your life, use what you can, and discard what does not feel right to you. There is no one on this planet better equipped to give you advice than you, so make sure you have conversations with yourself about what you read or hear. Then take what you need and get rid of the rest.

Realizing that you are the ultimate decision maker and you are the only one who has to live with every decision you make, will make your life a whole lot easier. Stop trying to make decisions for others and stop letting others make decisions for you. Get all the information you can and then go with your gut. We will talk about this in a later chapter so I won't say more than this right now. You are never wrong! Whatever decision you make is, in that moment, the best decision you can make based on the information you have at that time. Wow, that is powerful—you might want to reread that last sentence

Now that all the pressure is off, start making some of those decisions you have been putting off, and take action on those decisions right now.

If you take anything away from this chapter, take this: You are a rock star. You were born with awesome potential, and the fact that you are reading this book right now says to me that you are well on your way to realizing it. Not only are you the best at being you, you are the *only one* who can be you. And without you, our puzzle is not complete—not mine, not yours, and especially not your children's.

You are responsible for you and no one else is, so don't just blindly take advice, even from those who have what you want and have been where you are. Take the advice, think about it, and make the best decision for you in this moment. You are the one teacher who will teach you more than any other teacher over your lifetime. And remember, you are the only one who has to live with the decisions you will make throughout your lifetime.

The following are some questions that I suggest you ask yourself to get the most out of this chapter. Just make sure to take your time and really think about the answers.

1. Who am I listening to right now?
2. Who do I need to stop listening to?
3. Who do I want to start listening to?

CHAPTER 2

Why are you reading this book?

Why are you reading this book? I am going to take a stab at this based on the clients I currently work with as a life coach, sports coach, or business consultant. The people who usually come to me are looking to be better parents. They know they are capable of more; they just don't know how to do it. They come to me looking for answers to questions that they feel they have not been able to come up with on their own. If this is you, then I am going to spend the first part of this chapter talking directly to you. If this is not you, please don't skip this section because you may know someone like this and by reading this material you will be able to help them understand.

I grew up with parents who are loving and caring and absolutely did the best they could in raising all nine of their children. They did it pretty successfully, I might add, and that judgment is based solely on the results that my brothers, my sisters, and I have experienced in our lives. Still, like with myself and everyone else, there is always room for improvement. Not that they did anything wrong; I just know enough to know that there is always going to be a better way, a faster way, and easier way.

This is part of the journey I am on. I am always searching for a better way, and when I find it, I pass it on to everyone I have influence over. I want everyone to know what I know and realize the success that I have, or better yet, I want them to do better than I have done.

One of the reasons you are reading this book is that you are a lot like me. You want to be the best parent on the planet because you want to give your kids the best chance and the best start in their lives. This is what I like to call increasing their odds. Everything is about increasing your odds. You don't have to do all the things I suggest in this book, and you can be successful doing it your own way. I am just trying to increase your odds of success. You are still looking for that one nugget of gold that you know exists somewhere in one of these books you are reading, that one nugget that will make you a better parent and increase your child's chances of success in life. You are looking for that alternative that is going to give you a competitive advantage in life. You want more than what you currently have and because you want more, you know you can have more. You know inherently that there is more. There is something inside of you right now that is saying, "I know that I can do better". And you are absolutely right—you can do better, and you will.

Hopefully, you will find something on these pages that you can use in your life that makes you a better parent. You are a rock star, and I can say that with total confidence, without knowing who you are or anything else about you. I know you care, and that is the most important factor in you being a great parent. It all starts with you caring and asking the questions you have been asking yourself. When you ask the types of questions you have been asking yourself, you get the types of answers that will change your life and change your results. So keep asking those questions, and make sure you listen and look for the answers all around you. The Good Book says in Matthew 7:7, "Ask and it will be given to you." No question or prayer ever goes unanswered. So make sure you are asking a question that you really want the answer to.

If the preceding paragraphs did not feel like they were speaking to you, then you probably fall into this next category. You probably grew up in an environment where you quickly decided that you were not going to be like that when you became a parent. You might have grown up with less money or freedom than you wanted or you were constantly hearing the words, "We can't afford that" or "You can't do that." You lived a childhood that really allowed you to clarify what you wanted to be as a parent and what you wanted to provide for your children. You really just want your kids to have a better experience than you had growing up. You want them to have what you did not have access to as a kid. You want them to live a life that you feel is better than the one that you are living. You know there is more and so you want more for them.

You might have made some commitments to yourself that you were going to do things differently than your parents did. That you weren't going to be like them when you grew up and started your own family. Most people are a lot like you; they dream of a better life for themselves and their children. Where you stand out and are not like most people, is that you are doing something about it. I don't know how this book came to be in your possession. But I do know that there are no accidents and that this may just be one of the answers to one of your repeated prayers. I want you to know that although I do believe you can do better, I also know you are a good parent. You are doing what 90 percent of parents are not willing to do. You are here, reading this book, looking, searching for a new and better way. The good news is that what I am going to introduce you to throughout this book is not necessarily a better way, but it is definitely different from the approach that most parents take, and I have found it to be very effective in the raising of my three girls.

I know I have done a lot of talking and suggesting to you in this chapter as to the reason/reasons you are reading this book, and now it is time for you to do some thinking on your own. You don't have to, but I would suggest that you take a minute right here, right now, and answer this question: Why are you reading this book? Take as much time as you need to come up with an answer that feels good to you. Think about your answer and then write it down. Take out a white pad of paper and grab a pen. Take as much time as you need, and write the answer to this question.

Remember when I mentioned that whenever you ask a question it is always answered? If you will actually take the time right now to write out the answer to this question before you go on to the next chapter, the most amazing thing will occur. Your answer will actually determine what you get out of this book. You don't have to understand the preceding statement; just know that something magical happens when you go through this exercise. I want you to get the most out of this book, so do it now, don't wait. Put the book down and ask yourself this question: "Why am I reading this book?"

Take your time and write down your answer. Put it where you can reference it as you are reading this book. I might suggest even using it as your bookmark as you go through the book. What you will find in the book is exactly what you expect to find when you go through this exercise. You are more powerful than you can imagine, and soon I will take you on a journey of discovery that will change your perspective and give you a new lease on life. A life without limits for you and your children. Do it now. Put down the book and write down your answer to the above question. Then we will move on to the next chapter in our discussion.

Take a moment now, and write out your vision of where you want to be in five years. Really describe the person you will be when you see yourself living the life you are dreaming about right now. Make sure you describe the people you are with, your family, really get into as much detail as you possibly can.

Now, go and find the person who best represents, or most closely resembles the person you just described. Then ask him/her if they will mentor you. If you answer these questions, and follow these simple instructions, I promise you, you will look in the mirror five years from now, and you will be surprised by who you see staring back at you!

Something for you to consider before moving on to the next chapter.

1. Did you answer the question?

2. Did you write it down?

I can tell you will succeed beyond your own expectations because you are doing the work. Change starts with a thought, but only you will see this change until you act on that thought. You are a rock star!

CHAPTER 3

How to Turn "I can't" into "I will"

This is where we start to get into the fun stuff. I am so glad you took the time to do the exercise I suggested in the last chapter. Having completed that exercise, you will get so much more out of this book that you might even think this is the best book ever written, but I would suggest that it is not me, it's you who will make this the best book ever written.

For this chapter, we are going to have to go way back, I mean all the way back. We are going to have to travel back in time to when you were born. When you first entered into this world, you had no limitations. You were born with every talent and gift inside of you, and as you grew, your experiences, especially in your first seven years of life, helped you determine which talents you wanted to develop. And right up until the moment someone in a position of authority told you that you could not do something, you believed there was nothing you could not do. You were not afraid to try anything; you had no limitations.

I feel I should also mention that being told you could not do something is just one way you could have received your limitations or I should say, the *idea* that you have limitations. Another way is through your traumatic experiences. You felt invincible until one day you fell off the counter when your mother looked away for just a moment, and then you got hurt and you became afraid, afraid that you might get hurt again. Up until that moment, you were not afraid of anything.

The challenge now is that you find yourself afraid of other things too, totally unrelated to the incident, and these are not rational thoughts—instead, they come from your survival mechanism, your subconscious mind. In an effort to protect you from ever being hurt again, your subconscious mind has now introduced you to fear.

What is fear? Fear has been described to me as "False Evidence Appearing Real," and I like that, so let's go with it for now. Think about that—you can't see fear or touch fear. You can certainly feel fear, but is fear real? I would say no; it is only your subconscious mind trying to protect you from getting hurt.

This is the challenge: The number one reason you don't do something more, something greater than you are currently doing, is fear. You are afraid you might fail, and you are afraid of what people may think about you if you do fail. This one fear, which is never real, can be paralyzing. It can stop you in your tracks, and what happens when you stop moving forward? You start moving backward. You move to what you know and what you know is what your parents taught you. This is why so many children grow up to be just like their parents, many of whom swore that when they had kids they would not act like or do the same things that their parents did.

Why am I spending so much time on fear in this chapter when the title is, "How to turn 'I can't' into 'I will'"? The answer is simpler than you might think. The first and most common excuse that more than 90 percent of us use when we meet face-to-face with our fear is "I can't." Read the preceding sentence again— it contains something you will want to remember the next time you are attempting to do something and you start to feel fear.

You see, "I can't" is simply a cop out. It is the easy way out. Something looks hard, you are afraid of it, and so you say, "I can't do that." This somehow justifies to yourself your reason for not doing it. Looking at this written on this page, you might find yourself thinking there is no way it is that simple, but I would suggest to you that it is. Think about that one for a moment before you move on.

So what's the answer? How do I turn "I can't" into "I will"? Easy, just eliminate fear from your life. Wait, what did he just say? Yes, you heard right, eliminate fear from your life. Fear is not real, so why make it a part of your life? Fear was put into your mind to keep you safe, and most of us would agree that in today's world there is far less to worry about than there was maybe ten thousand years ago. I would suggest that you take the acronym I gave you for fear, "False Evidence Appearing Real," and use it. Make it your mantra, because if you do, your whole life will change.

There is no better place to experience this than in the world of extreme sports. We call it extreme sports because we are afraid to participate in them. Do you realize that? The athletes who participate in these sports spend hours of time and practice calculating risk versus reward and refining their skills until they can say with certainty that they will make the thing they are attempting possible. They calculate wind speed, distance, velocity, and many other variables, but one thing they do not include in the equation is fear. Why is that? Because they know better than most that fear is not real. Therefore, it should not be entered into the equation.

I want to share with you something I tell my young athletes when I am training them. I think it could be helpful to you if you adopt this in your life. You have often heard of an athlete having the butterflies right before they go up to bat, or run out on the field, or get ready to attempt a high dive. What you have probably been told is that those are your nerves, which is true, but it is only part of the story. The feeling that we commonly refer to as "the butterflies" is your nerves getting you ready for what your body knows you are about to do. It is not a bad thing, in fact it is just the opposite—it is a good thing. Your body is so incredible that it prepares for an activity in advance of that activity. It knows, through experience, what it will be expected to do in just a few moments, so it is preparing for the moment.

Think about this for a second: If you were told from an early age what those "butterflies" really were, would you have done more? If you were not afraid, would you have been able to accomplish more and take more risks to achieve your goals? Of course you would have, and so would the rest of us. What probably happened is that someone early in your life said that you were just nervous and you should just get over it and go ahead with what you were doing and you would be fine.

Let's take a quick survey here. Raise your hand if that *ever* made you feel better. You are probably not raising your hand right now because it has been my experience that explaining your feelings at that moment in that way never made anyone feel better. So why do so many people still say that, even to this day? The answer is simple—they don't know the rest of the story. They don't know what you now know.

In summary of this chapter, let's review exactly how we can turn "I can't" into "I will." The first thing you must do is realize that fear is not real. Fear is something your mind created and those around you have perpetuated through your life up until now. The second thing you must do is realize that your body is one of, if not the most, advanced technologies on the planet. And if a computer can predict and project things into the future based on the past and the data that has been fed to it, is it so hard to believe that your body, which is far more advanced than any computer, can do the same thing? So the next time your child is "nervous" about something, let them know that it is their body getting them ready for the amazing thing they are about to do.

Now before we finish, let's talk about the words you use every day. This is critical, and I would be remiss if I left it out of this chapter. What you say matters because what you say is a direct reflection of what you are thinking, and what you are thinking determines what you do, and what you do determines what habits you create, and it's your habits that create the results you are getting in your life. Instead of saying, "I can't," say something like, "At this moment, I am not able to." Instead of telling your child "You can't have that," say something like "Right now we are saving for a new home, and your choosing not to have that right now will allow you to get so much more from our new home and your new room". This of course is going to have to be personalized by you to your situation, and hopefully you get the point.

What you say matters, and what you say a lot matters even more. Think of your child as a sponge. This is what allows children to learn so fast in their early years, up until about seven or eight years old. They have no filter; what you tell them sticks, so make sure you are telling them only things you know will benefit them for their lifetime. If you are going to say something that could limit them, exercise self-control and don't say it. Reframe everything you say to have the same result, but the energy around it will not create a belief in your children that could limit them for the rest of their lifetime.

Take a moment here and reflect on some of the things you have said to your child over the last twenty-four hours. Were the things you said empowering or disempowering? If they were empowering, good, you are on the right track. If they were disempowering, you might want to reconsider what you are telling your kids.

Now is a good time to mention that it is not just what you say to your children directly that affects them; in fact, what you say to others in front of your children has far more influence on how they think and act than what you tell them directly.

When I have had this conversation with many parents in the past, they are quick to say they would never say those disempowering things to their child, and then moments later they are saying it to a friend as they are participating in "harmless" gossip while in earshot of their child.

I am sure you have heard the saying, "Kids don't do what you say, they do what you do." If you have not, then let me repeat it here, "Kids don't do what you say, they do what you do." And if you are talking with someone else, you are doing something your children are more likely to mimic and repeat than if you are talking directly to your children.

So how can I turn "I can't" to "I will"?

First, watch your words. Keep a log of everything that you say to your kids, or anyone else over the next 24 hours. Make it simple, you don't even need to write down the thing you say, simply make a T chart. Draw a horizontal line on a piece of paper near the top of the paper. Then draw a vertical line right down the center of your paper, start this line just above the horizontal line you drew in the last step, and travel all the way to the bottom of your paper. On the left side of the vertical line, and above the horizontal line, write the word, "Empowering". On the right side of the vertical line, and again above the horizontal line, write the word "Disempowering". Fold the paper and put it in your pocket. For the next 24hrs every time you say something empowering put a tally mark in the left column of your chart. Every time you say something limiting, or disempowering, put a tally mark in that column.

At the end of 24hrs, check in and see how you did. The side with the most tally marks wins. Now, based on your results, are you empowering or disempowering your children? Hopefully this exercise will be a real eye opener for you.

Now, decide to do better, I know you can! You are a rock star!

CHAPTER 4

A Life Without Limits

This is one of the more exciting chapters in this book. I absolutely love talking about this and especially with young athletes who usually have high hopes and aspirations. My mission in life is to empower children to achieve in life, and I do that through sports. I am going to share an analogy I use all the time, and it has served me well in keeping my mind focused on what's important.

When I am talking about the potential of our children with parents, I like to use the following analogy: Our children are like a bucket, and we fill that bucket constantly with good or bad filler, whatever that may be. Let's pretend we have a bucket, and it is sitting in a grass field, and we also have a hose that has an unlimited supply of water.

Once we turn on the hose and the water starts flowing, there is no way to turn it off. The water will continue to fill the bucket forever. As parents, we sometimes, usually unknowingly, put a lid on the bucket, and the pressure inside keeps building and building until finally it explodes and water goes everywhere. Now this may sound like a bad thing, but let's dive a little deeper.

When the bucket explodes and water goes everywhere, what do you think happens to the grass all around the bucket? It turns green. That's right, it turns green. Sometimes we put a lid on our children, but it can only be temporary because you can only keep a lid on that bucket until the pressure inside exceeds the pressure on the outside. At that moment, your child will change the world around him or her.

What I am going to suggest is that you never put the lid on. Then the pressure doesn't build up inside, and your child is allowed to change the world sooner and faster. The grass around the bucket is affected before it has a chance to die and greens up quicker. The reach of the water flowing out of the bucket is farther, therefore making more green grass.

Your child is special and unique. There is not one other child like him/her on the planet. Treat your child as if this is so, and you will see something happen that is more amazing than you can now imagine.

If you have put a lid on your children, don't wait. Begin taking it off right now. Do what you can to let them know that whatever their dream is, it is meant for them to accomplish. In fact, you might want to let them know that because they have been blessed with that dream, it is their duty to make it come true. There are people in this world who need that dream as much or more than they do, and because they are unique and special, they are the only ones who can make that dream a reality. A lot of grass will go unwatered if they live their entire life without realizing their dream.

Wow, that gets me every time. I love telling that story. I can imagine that your face was lighting up as you were reading it, just like I have seen with so many parents before you, and their eyes lit up when I told them this story. A life without limits is what we are all born with. We have the ability to choose if we are going to live that life or if we are going to restrict ourselves.

I am teaching you this now so that you can take the off your kid and see what he or she can do. I have known my children their entire lives, and there is not one single day that goes by that I am not amazed by something they say or do. And if you stop to think about it right now, you will find the same to be true with your children. Really think about this for a moment. I often say that the most I have ever learned in my life was taught to me by my children, and if more people were open to that one thought, they would see the greatness in their children as well.

The greatest gift I have ever received in my life was the gift of fatherhood. I truly believe that, and I am thankful every day for that privilege. Too many times as parents, we assume that since we have been on this planet longer than our children, we automatically know better. I want to suggest to you right now that time is not a qualifier when determining knowledge. What I mean by that is this: Just because you have been doing something for a long time does not mean that you are qualified to teach it. You may have been doing it one way the whole time, and someone else has been doing it a totally different way and experiencing a much more promising result. I think this bears repeating: Time is not a qualifier.

Some of the most inspirational words I have ever heard were also the simplest, and they came from my children and from other children I have had contact with. Listen to your kids; they will teach you something new every day, and you will be amazed at what they know compared to what you know.

As we come to the end of this chapter, I will leave you with the following thought:

A life without limits starts with the most influential person in a child's life, and that person is you. You have the capability to facilitate a longer, happier life for your child by allowing him or her to be who they are and to experience what they are here to experience. A life without limits is not only possible; it is a reality for more and more of our children every day. With your help, we will guide these kids to living a life without limits, and it is they who will change the world. If you really want to make a difference in this world, tell your child every day how special he/she is and remind them that with that power comes a great responsibility to live a long and full life.

It is our children who are going to bring peace to this world. We are just the facilitators of their dreams when they are still in our care. They will accomplish great things, with or without our help. I am simply suggesting that with our help, they will do it faster!

An exercise you can and should do with your children to drive this chapter home.

Do this exercise with your children. And participate! It is more effective if you do it with them, than if you just introduce it to them, and have them do it. Make a game out of this, make it fun for you and your kids. Who has the biggest dream in your family? Give a prize to the biggest dreamer. And everyone will win! Now, for the instructions:

Take your kids to the store and have them pick out a notebook that is special to them. The more colorful or the more beautiful the pictures are on the cover of the notebook, the better. Now, buy them a pen with blue ink. The same rules apply to the pen as the notebook, the cooler it is the better their experience will be with this exercise.

Pick a day of the week that you are going to do this, any day, and make sure it is a day that you can do this exercise every week. I want you to do this with them every week, and make it fun so that they look forward to it. Consistency is the key to this exercise. The first time you sit down, your task will be to decorate the notebooks. You can draw pictures, add stickers, color pages in the note book, or anything else you and your amazing kids come up with. Remember, each person, and every child is unique, however they choose to decorate the book is perfect, don't be the judge, just let the creativity flow! A suggestion for the title of the notebook would be "My Dream Book" or "My Vision Book", whatever they decide to call it, is perfect! Draw the title in big letters, or spell it out in stickers, whatever they want.

Week 2, and every week after that, these are the instructions for what to put in the notebook. First, set the scene by asking them this question: (maybe even have them write this on the inside cover of the book) "If money was no object and you could have, be and do anything you wanted, what would you have, be and do?" Remember, money is no object, for this exercise, there are no limits other than those of your imagination. Then allow them to free flow their thoughts, and if you need to use the following as general guidelines:

There are no limits, if they can think it, they can write it

1. Money is no object
2. No dream is too big
3. No dreamer is too small

Have fun, run with it, it's your imagination!

CHAPTER 5

What Is Your Purpose?

———

You might ask, "What is this doing here, in the middle of a book on parenting?" Do you remember in a previous chapter when I mentioned that our children do not do what we say, they do what we do? If you are not living a purpose-driven life, how can you expect that of them? We all want our kids to succeed and live a purpose-driven life, but someone along the way suggested that we had to settle, life was hard, and we should just accept that, and in accepting that advice (from a person most likely who was not qualified to give it) we stopped living our purpose.

I will tell you right now that in all my years of playing organized sports I have seen coaches who are very effective and win a lot, and I have seen coaches who are not. Let me regress a little and explain why because I think this is an appropriate time to do so.

When you are coaching your children or young athletes or anyone, sometimes they require your belief that something works until they prove to themselves that it works. If you have not done or cannot not do what you are trying to coach someone to do, how strong is your belief that it will work? I would suggest that it is probably not strong enough to pull you along and your students with you.

If you have done something yourself and experienced the results of it working, you know it works; it is no longer a belief. And it is only when you know something works that you are strong enough to support those whom you are teaching through that first part of the learning process or the success cycle (which we will talk about in great detail in a later chapter) until they establish in themselves the belief that something works. Let me give you a real example from my experience.

I have been coaching baseball in the Denver Metro area for more than sixteen years as of the time of writing this book, and a good friend of mine has also coached for about the same amount of time. He has played baseball as long as I have and has experienced success in one facet of the game. When he coaches a team, the trouble is that he is not very good at most of the game, just that one facet. So how can he convince a young athlete that what he knows works if they cannot see it, or better yet, feel that belief in him. He says what most people would consider to be all the right things, and they sound good coming out of his mouth. But they lack substance—the belief behind the words is missing, and therefore his words fall on deaf ears more times than not.

I can come in front of the same team and say the exact same things word for word, and I will experience a different result with the team. I have spent so many years developing and understanding all facets of the game, and I can perform in all the positions on the field at a high level. Because of that, my belief in what I am teaching has reached the level of "knowingness." Knowingness means you have a belief that has become an unconscious awareness; for example, you know that the sun will come up tomorrow. The athletes I teach can feel that and use it for their benefit until they see that it works for themselves.

If you believe anything I just said, you now know why your children are or are not living a life with purpose. It is for no other reason than because the person they most look up to in this world is—or is not—living his or her purpose. Don't get me wrong, kids are resilient, and they will do what they have to do to live their dreams. All I am saying is that if you do the things I suggest, you are going to greatly increase their odds of winning at the game of life. And that's really what this book and what parenting are all about—increasing their odds of making it.

So let's shift gears back again and re-ask the question I asked at the beginning of this chapter. What is your purpose? It's okay if you don't remember, it may have been a while since you have even thought about this question. Don't beat yourself up about it; let's discover it together through a process I am about to give you.

This process is not mine, by the way. It is adapted from Mark Hamilton, and I strongly recommend reading any of his works, as he is a real thought leader and pioneer in the world of human potential. The first question I would ask you is, What do you do on Friday nights? What I mean by this is what do you do to relax, unwind, and get away from work? I am not talking about having a drink with your friends at the bar, so for now let's leave that one out of the equation.

What I am really looking for is what do you do in your free time, which currently you do not get paid for, but you do anyway? Usually I get answers like, "I play baseball, I coach my kids' team, I run," or things like that. Most people don't know you can make money doing anything, and whatever you do in your free time that you currently do not get paid for, you would probably be really good at if you did it full time, and the icing on the cake is when you do that, you get paid for it.

This is usually the area in which you have the most talent, experience, and love and passion for. This becomes the basis for your purpose. When you live on purpose, the world becomes your playground, and every day becomes a new adventure. If that sounds good to you at all, imagine how that sounds to your child.

Now do you see why we are talking about this right here? If you are not living your purpose, it is going to be very hard to convince your children to live theirs, which is one of the reasons you are reading this book. You want more from life for your kids than you have yourself.

You can also discover your hidden talents by making a list of your hobbies and things you like to do for fun. Look closely at what they are and what talents or skills it takes to do those activities. It is likely, if not one hundred percent certain, that there is a job out there that requires those skills, and it would leave you more fulfilled than you are now if you were doing it.

I would also suggest that it would be easy for you to go to work every day, you would love what you do, and you would likely be really good at it! The challenge I find with a lot of parents I work with is that they believe they are limited in the ways they can make money to what they are doing currently or the field they are currently working in. This sounds like more of the fear, and "I can't" mentality to me.

Now that your perception and thinking have changed just a little bit, I would encourage you to make a list, check it twice, and discover the hidden talents in you. Then take that information and make a change in your life. Start living on purpose, and you will be surprised at how quickly your kids pick up on the example you are setting in your home. They will start to know how much fun it is to live on purpose and see that they can make a difference in this world.

We are all blessed with the seeds of talents and abilities, and it is our choice to develop the talents we choose based on our desires. We then develop them through our life experiences. There is no more powerful example for our children than for us to be leading a purpose-driven life. The example we set for our kids will change the course of their lives forever, and we will all be having fun along the way.

Take the time to develop a purpose, and then make a commitment to yourself and to your kids to live it. Live it every day and in every way. That means living life on purpose—with direction, passion, and an end goal in mind.

You will see a change in them that cannot be taken back. Your children will accomplish things daily that you would not have believed they could accomplish in their lifetimes before. You will play together more and grow closer as a family because you will be so much more connected.

Living on purpose will not fix everything in your life and make you a perfect parent, but it will go a long way toward making you the best parent you can possibly be.

How do I start living my life on purpose?

Ok, time to start living your life on purpose. Do the following exercise to figure out what your life purpose might be:

Make a list of the things you enjoy the most. Don't hold back, and don't judge anything, for now just write down everything that you love to do.

Now, go through your list and pick the top five things that you just can't live without, you absolutely love to do these things. Then, do the research. Take each of the top five items on your list and research all the ways that you can think of that people are getting paid to do those things. Google will be your new best friend for this exercise. You just might be surprised at what you really can do, for which you will get paid.

After you have done the research, sit down and determine your top prospect, or your next logical step. Use the following questions to guide you in this process:

1. What is the compensation range? Example: $25 hour to $25,000 a show, or $1million a show.

Once you have decided on the one that feels the best to you, ask the following questions:

1. Who do I have access to who is currently doing this? (access can be someone you know, or a book written by someone doing this, or classes

that teach you how to make a business out of your passion, anything really).

If you chose a person who is still alive, write them a letter. You can structure this letter any way you want, and if it were me, I would structure it like Napoleon Hill suggests in his book "The Law of Success". Below is a copy of the letter from that book.

Hon. Thomas R. Marshall,
Vice President of the United States, Washington, D.C.

My dear Mr. Marshall:

Would you care for the opportunity to send a message of encouragement, and possibly a word of advice, to a few hundred thousand of your fellowmen who have failed to make their mark in the world as successfully as you have done?

I have about completed a manuscript for a book to be entitled "How to Sell Your Services." The main, point made in the book is that service rendered is cause and the pay envelope is effect: and that the latter varies in proportion to the efficiency of the former.

The book would be incomplete without a few words of advice from a few men who, like yourself, have come up from the bottom to enviable positions in the world. Therefore, if you will write me of your views as to the most essential points to be borne in mind by those who are offering personal services for sale, I will pass your message on through my book, which will insure its getting into hands where it will do a world of good for a class of earnest people who are struggling to find their places in the world's work.

I know you are a busy man, Mr. Marshall, but please bear in mind that by simply calling in your secretary and dictating a brief letter you will be sending forth an important message to possibly half a million people. In money, this will not be worth to you the two-cent stamp that you will place on the letter, but, if estimated from the viewpoint of the good it may do others who are less fortunate than yourself, it may be worth the difference between success and failure to many a worthy person who will read your message, believe in it, and be guided by it.

Very cordially yours.

Yes, I think if any of us got that letter, we would do what was asked of us. This was written a long time ago, but if you really want change, and you find someone who has what you want, isn't it worth your time to study the style and format that this letter is written in? Then you will greatly increase your odds of getting the mentorship you want.

CHAPTER 6

How Coachable Are You?

———

I t's time to test the water and see where you are in this learning process. You may have heard this before, and I think most teachers ask the question, "How teachable are you?" Coachable and teachable mean the same thing. I have just translated the word into my coach's lingo.

I love this part of the process, because this is where information is translated into action. Depending on how coachable you are, you may already be seeing results from the information you have been given in this book. For example, if you have done all of the exercises in this book so far, you are probably very coachable. If you have done none of the exercises so far, you are probably not coachable at all. There is a direct relationship between your coachability and your results. One of my mentors explains the teachability index as follows:

The first part is on a scale of one to ten, what is your willingness to learn? One being the lowest and you don't want to learn anything new, and ten being the highest and you are open to learning anything that will move you forward. The second part is on a scale of one to ten, what is your willingness to accept change? One being the lowest, you don't want to change anything, and ten being the highest, you want everything to change. When you answer those two questions, you multiply your answers together and that gives you your teachability index score (coach-ability).

If, for example, on a scale of one to ten you are a one, and you don't want to learn anything new, and on your willingness to change you are a ten, then you would multiply one times ten and your index score would be a ten. Ten may seem good, but if we are talking about ten out of a possible one hundred, then you are not very teachable and you will not have any success in implementing what I am teaching you in this book. You will not have success because you will put this book back on your shelf, forget you read it, and move on without taking any action on anything I suggest. If on the other hand, you take the test and you are a ten and a ten, ten times ten is one hundred, you are the highest and most coachable and you will take action on everything I suggest to you in this book and you will see dramatic change in the results you are currently achieving in your life. In return, you will see a dramatic change in your kids' lives as a result of your change.

This index is dynamic, meaning that it is always changing. It can change from minute to minute, or chapter to chapter, and you have to constantly check in if you feel push-back or reluctance to the information you are reading and see how coachable you are. I will give you a great example of this from a few years ago when I was attending a week-long event in Canada hosted by none other than Bob Proctor himself. Bob has been called a Master Thinker and has been studying the human mind for more than fifty years. He is an author, speaker, trainer, and thought leader, and is a student of Napoleon Hill.

At the time, I had been a student of Bob's work for about a year and was super excited to go and see him live and get the opportunity to learn from him face-to-face. Then when I was sitting at the table in the room on the first day of the week-long event, I found myself having major push-back on one of the first topics he was discussing. I asked myself if I was being coachable in that moment and the answer was a resounding no. I knew that Bob had something I wanted and that this was going to be a wasted week if I was not open to receiving the information he had for me.

I then took a moment, walked around outside, and looked at things in the distance for a few minutes. I focused on noticing what was going on around me and then calmed down and grounded myself. I walked back into the event and found that I was much more open and receptive to the information, and that week ended up changing the course of my life entirely.

I would not be writing this book right now had I not been coachable while Bob was up there on stage speaking to us about our paradigms and how we had to shift them if we were going to experience change in our lives.

I am not saying that everything I have to offer you on the pages of this book is gold. All I am saying is that if you are not open to any of it, you will not get what you want out of it. And the whole reason I am sitting here writing this book is for you. I want you to become more aware and empowered to make the changes in your life that will in turn make the changes in your children's lives that you are looking for.

All I am asking is that you take in the information, think about it, use what you want, and throw away the rest. You are not going to agree with everything I write in here, and I don't expect you to. I just don't want that to stop you from learning something that could change the course of your life.

Hopefully you now have at least a basic understanding of what it means to be coachable. I know lots of people in the personal development world who tell me all the time how coachable they are, and yet their experience remains the same. The one thing I know to be true is that if your environment is not changing and your results are not changing, then you are not coachable, and you are not changing, no matter how much you talk about it.

Remember, it's not what you say, it's what you do that your kids remember. It is also true that it's not what you *talk about* that gets you results in life; it's what you *do* that gets the results. You can go to see some of the most influential people on the planet for years and years, and you can tell your friends how much you love them, but if you don't have the results in your life that you want, it comes down to one thing—you are not coachable. If someone has what you want and they are teaching you what they did to get it, and they were at one point where you are, then there is only one thing stopping you from getting the results you want—you are not coachable.

Let me share with you two examples from my experience as a coach that show you both ends of the spectrum: what happens when you are not coachable, and what happens when you are the most coachable. I was coaching for a high school baseball team when a young talented freshman came into our program and we had a lot of high expectations for this young man. He was a super talent and was the star of his team growing up, no matter who he played for. You could tell that it just came easily to him at that point. He made varsity his first year as a starting pitcher. He did pretty well.

Everything was looking good for him, then he started to not show up all the time to practice, and he wasn't putting forth a lot of effort. What was happening was that he believed he did not need practice, and he was too good for it. He was not coachable at all. Over his next three years his performance stayed about the same. The difference was all of his competition was getting better at the same time he was staying the same. His senior year he lost his starting position and rode the bench most of the year. He could not understand because he was the same talented young man who came in with all that potential as a freshman and then never did anything with it. Because he thought he was too good to be taught, he did not change, and the whole time he was busy not changing, everyone around him was getting better, and those who were behind him when he started were soon ahead of him.

Now I want to tell you about a young man who was on a fourteen-U (fourteen and under age bracket) competitive team I coached. I only coached the team for two seasons. The first season was his first season ever playing baseball. On the first day of practice in introductions, I earned his respect and admiration almost immediately as someone who had what he wanted. He was a ten and a ten, so he had a coachability index of one hundred. Everything I said to him he remembered. Everything I suggested he do on his own time to improve he did.

I couldn't wait to see him at every practice because he was improving so fast that I just wanted to know where he was. This brings up another principle that we will talk about in much more detail in a later chapter. Enthusiasm, no matter what causes it, creates a more lasting impact and a greater change than any other emotion.

After just two seasons this young man moved on to play for a more competitive team and is still coachable and still getting better every time I see him. To put it bluntly, if you want to succeed in life, be coachable. There is always something more for you to learn, and the only way to do that is to be coachable.

Ok, it's time to check in with yourself

Be honest, because anything short of that will not create the change in your life that you are looking for. Please answer the following questions openly and honestly:

1. Are you willing and open to listen to new information?
2. Are you willing to learn new ideas?
3. Have you done any or all the exercises in this book so far?
4. What are you willing to do to get what you want?
5. Are you willing to do whatever it takes?

CHAPTER 7

How Do You Lead?

———

In all of my years coaching I would have to say that in parenting styles I have run into more dictators than I have guidance counselors. The challenge with this is easily seen when you think back to what I said in an earlier chapter. If you put a lid on your kid, you will hold him or her back. That being said, if you try to dictate how they are to live their lives instead of simply giving them guidance, then you are putting that lid on them. You are trying to control something you don't understand. You think you do because you have lived your life, you know how this works, you have been there and done that. You have made mistakes and you want to make sure that your kids don't make those same mistakes, I get that.

What I want you to understand and really just be aware of, is that there may be a better way. This is where the title of this book comes from, *Coaching the Home Team*. I want to teach you how to be a coach and sometimes even a mentor to your kids because that can be much more valuable in their development than being a dictator over them.

I am a firm believer in evolution. Now before you pass judgement on that statement, let me explain what I mean by that. You see, I believe that every evolution of a flower is better than the previous, every version of the iPhone is better than the one before it, and every evolution of the family is better than the one before it. So if I believe all this to be true, how could I possibly tell my kids what to do? According to this concept, they are better than I am, and I truly believe that. I am not here to tell them what to do; I am here to share with them my experiences and let them know what I have learned and then stand back and allow them to make their own choices based on their current perspective.

I know some of you are thinking, Wait a minute, JT, I know better than they do, and I have to make the decisions for them so they don't get hurt. I would suggest that the opposite is true: The more decisions you make for them, the worse it's going to be when they do start making their own because you will have denied them the experience of making their own decisions.

I can only share my own experiences from being a parent and coach for all these years, and that experience tells me that when set free from my restraints, these kids make better decisions than I could have ever made for them. I still get caught in the trap of thinking I know what's best for my girls sometimes, but because they are so used to making their own decisions, they are very quick to thank me for my input and then politely ask me to step back while they make their own decisions.

This is exactly what I was talking about in an earlier chapter when I mentioned that my kids are my greatest teachers. I don't do it as much anymore because I am learning, but I used to constantly underestimate what they were capable of. For the record, at the time of the writing of this book, my twelve-year-old daughter has been invited to the inauguration of our new president in January of 2017, and she currently teaches a small class on Thursday nights on how to make money in the stock market.

Here is the thing: Expectations are powerful, and when you set high expectations for your children and allow them to do the same, watch out—you have no idea what they can do, and I promise you, it is so much more than you are currently giving them credit for. I don't want to get off of the subject here, but I am going to mention that I believe this is why our school system is so ineffective right now. From day one the system places all children into the same category, slaps labels on them, and then teaches them all the same as if they are robots that just need to be programmed.

If you believe anything I have suggested to you so far in this book, you can clearly see the fault in that type of instruction and thinking. That's like saying, "You are the most incredible child on the planet, and I know what's best for you, so sit still, do your work, and don't talk back."

"Wait, didn't you just say I was the most incredible child on the planet? What then gives you the right to make my choices for me?"

Okay, let's get back to the focus of this book—coaching the home team. I want to suggest that the reason a good coach gets so much more out of his/her players is because he/she coaches them. Instead of dictating or judging, the good coach encourages and guides. He or she gives them tools that, if used properly, will ensure their success.

Good coaches put them in a position on the field for which they are best suited to succeed. Who decides what position that is, by the way? Your children, of course. They always do and always will know what is best for them in that moment. By empowering your children to make decisions for themselves starting at an early age, they naturally become better decision makers. They have a better head on their shoulders. They don't always get better grades in school, but that's okay because school is not meant for everyone. What they do always do is make better decisions for themselves.

Have you ever known parents who, as soon as they turn their back, their child does something against their wishes? On the opposite side, have you ever known a parent whose child behaves the same whether the parent is looking or not? The difference is that the first parent makes all the decisions for their child, so as soon as they are left on their own, they make poor decisions because they are not good decision makers—they have no practice. On the other hand, the child whose parents allow him/her to make their own decisions, is well practiced and very good at making decisions on their own.

I mentioned this earlier, but I want to say again here that age does not matter. Your child is born with the ability to make decisions, and the sooner you allow him or her to start developing that ability, the better they get at it. Practice makes perfect, right? You have to give them a chance to practice while you are around to guide them. That way, when you turn them loose on their own, they have had years of practice ahead of time in making their own decisions, and they will of course make better decisions on the fly.

I know that this chapter can be a tough pill to swallow for a lot of parents. It seems to go against traditional parenting. It is definitely a different idea. I don't want to say it's better or worse, it's just different. I think if you are open to this idea and you take it home and implement it in your home, you will be pleasantly surprised with the results. I have had numerous parents come up to me and question me on this idea and then immediately tell me all the reasons why their son/daughter is totally unqualified to make decisions on their own.

The only answer I have for that is sometimes a tough pill to swallow: "How do you know? Based on what you just said, you have never given them the chance." They usually then tell me about the times their kids were given a chance to make a decision on their own and they messed up, and when asked more about the situation, they talk about a decision that was made when their back was turned.

Remember what I said earlier: If they don't get any practice while you are looking at them, they will not make good decisions when you are not looking at them. If anything, their argument against my line of thinking actually proves me to be correct. I just want you to know that every child has an emotional guidance system built in. It is kind of like their internal GPS, and when it is allowed to be developed, it works better and better as they grow.

Teach them how to go with their gut and make decisions on their own, and guide them through that process. Not only will they have a good life, but you as a parent will have a much easier go of it.

Ask yourself the following questions:

1. Do I give my child the opportunity to make decisions, or do I make them for him/her?

2. When was the last time they made a good decision without me?

3. What can I change right now to help my child learn to be a good decision maker?

4. Am I ready to let him/her shine?

CHAPTER 8

The "I Look Good" Drill

———

I developed this drill a few years ago when coaching a group of kids who were brought together because they did not have the ability or talent to make the teams they had tried out for. There were enough of them that the parents called me and asked if I would coach them. I accepted and it was one of the most amazing experiences of my life. I learned so much from them.

One of the things I noticed when doing my initial assessments of my players was that they had something in common that I would consider a failure trait. They all lacked confidence in their abilities as a person, let alone as a baseball player. When doing my assessment, I found that most of them were not doing well in school, and a lot of them were going out for baseball because they kind of liked it, but mostly because their parents wanted them to participate in a sport that would keep them away from their siblings for long enough to hopefully reduce the amount of fighting that was going on between them. There were some other behavioral issues that they were dealing with, but this covers most of what I found.

I knew what those kids needed the most was a strong boost of self-confidence. You see, our society has it a little backwards; often we hear people telling us we should keep our egos in check, or we should not show off. I say this is one of the most counterproductive things you could ever say to your child. Cherish your prima donnas. You want your child to be confident and able to lead and make decisions on their own. You want them to take control of their lives and any situation that they are in. You love to see it, so support that, and not the opposite of that.

Confidence is a key part in the success cycle, which we will talk about in depth in a later chapter. Without confidence you do not take action and without action you do not accomplish anything. I knew I needed a way to help this team with their confidence before I could do anything else. And thus was born what I call the "I Look Good" drill.

When I am instructing players, I break down all fundamentals into singular movements and create checkpoints for them as they move through the exercise so that they can tell where they are messing up based on the results they are getting from the drill. So the

I Look Good drill fit perfectly and naturally into my process of teaching.

What I did was instruct the players to go through the drill step by step, and at each checkpoint look at their mechanics, and if they looked good, they were to simply state "I look good." You can imagine what a powerful impact this has on kids who have little or no confidence. I would guess that they said "I look good" at least a hundred times every single practice during our different drills. It was amazing.

Their confidence as individuals and as a team grew slowly at first and then seemingly overnight they all grew confident. Imagine for a moment if you stood in front of the mirror every morning and you repeated "I look good" a hundred times. You may not believe it at first, but eventually you would be convinced that you look good, and once you were convinced that you looked good, you would feel good. Amazingly simple, yet super effective. Try it with your kids. It works every time. Just stick to it.

You can have a lot of fun with this one. For instance, I make it a point every time I see my girls to mention how they somehow manage to get cuter every single day. I always make it a point to let them know that I am taking notice of their constant improvement. Just by simply practicing this every day, they have over time developed so much confidence that they not only have a ton of friends, but as mentioned in an earlier chapter of this book, my twelve-year-old teaches a class on how to trade the stock market.

The part I did not mention was that her confidence was born after she attended an event in Atlanta and spoke on stage in front of four hundred people and presented her research on a company she wanted to buy. When you raise your child's level of confidence, you change their world. Talk about a life without limits.

Another great example is my middle daughter. She was having trouble with a bully at school and initially our response as parents was to report the incident and have a teacher handle it, but then I thought about it and decided that was not going to solve the problem for our daughter. I sat down with her and we discussed at length what was going on and she came up with a solution that I thought was so crazy and simple that I knew it would work.

What she came up with was a smile chart for her. She would make a conscious effort to smile more, and she tracked it on an index card. Every time she would smile, she would pull the index card out of her pocket and put a tally mark on it. The incentive I added for her was that I would give her fifty dollars if she reached a certain number of smiles per day on average. I also suggested that whenever she saw the bully, she would smile at her and pull out the index card.

Soon after, everything changed for my daughter. She was happier, the bully was still around but no longer bothering her, her friends were now keeping track of their smiles, and at a parent teacher conference her teacher asked what was going on because she had noticed a difference in Mylee and her behavior. Mylee started getting along better in school, her grades improved, and I can trace all this back to her smile chart. Because she was constantly smiling and monitoring that, her demeanor changed, and when her demeanor changed, her confidence rose because of the improved interactions she was having with fellow students, teachers, bus drivers, and everyone she came in contact with. It was one of the most incredible things I have ever witnessed.

She is currently developing a smile tracker app and will be releasing it soon. In fact, by the time you are reading this book it may already be out, so look it up and have your kids download it. Then track the change in their level of confidence; you will be pleasantly surprised.

Let's wrap this chapter up by having you create your own I look good drill for your kids.

You can do it. You have the basic concept here in this chapter, if you need to, read it again. Sit down with your kids and guide them into coming up with their own ideas, like Mylee, they know what will work best for them, sometimes you need to coach it out of them. Then set up a tracking system, and an accountability system. You want to make sure that it covers at least one month. This will develop in your child a new habit, and this new habit will change their results and confidence dramatically. Don't waste another minute, do it now. Schedule a family sit down, or do it one on one with each individual child, develop a game, a tracking system, and a way that they can be held accountable. Then implement it. Put your plan into action right away, and don't sit there and think that you will do it next week, or after you finish reading this book, because statistics show that if you don't act on this item within the next forty-eight hours, you will likely never act on it. All the information and knowledge in the world will do you no good, and create no change in your life if you never act on it. And real change cannot take place until you form a new habit, and habits are formed by repeating an action repeatedly consciously until you no longer need think about it, you just do it. So, do it, sit down, make a plan, and implement it right now before you move on to the next chapter. How coachable are you right now?

A few general guidelines for creating your own "I look good" drill:

1. Make it something they already do every day.
2. Choose something that has at least five different actions.
3. Choose something that they usually do in front of a mirror.

Example: brushing your teeth

Really get emotionally involved in this exercise. If it was me, I would make it over the top funny. Below is an example of what the first step in brushing your teeth might look like.

As I look into the mirror, say out loud the following, while smiling big and proud at the person in the mirror;

"Wow, I really look good. I mean, look at that fantastic smile, imagine what it will look like after I get done brushing my teeth!"

Make sure you go through every step of the teeth brushing process. The next step might sound like this:

"Wow, what a great toothbrush I have, this pink tooth brush really makes my smile look good!"

Now, you have the general idea, go have fun with this!

CHAPTER 9

The Success Cycle

Y ou may or may not have heard of the success cycle. Either way, my objective in this chapter is to explain it to you in such a simple way that you can pass this information on to your child. You will find that once this has been explained to you as simply as I will do here, you will begin to see it in everything you look at. You will notice it in nature, in traffic, at the game, in your home, in the movies, and everywhere you go. You will begin to see it in the news and world events. You will see it in the stories you read and most importantly you will recognize it in your own life. So let's get started.

The success cycle is also commonly referred to as the momentum cycle, and most teachers talk to you about the success cycle in one direction. What most of them fail to do is tell you what happens in the success cycle if you are not moving forward. One of my friends and mentors used to tell me that if you're not growing, you're dying. What he meant is that we are not living in a static universe. Our world is constantly changing and improving, so even if we were standing still and resting on our laurels, what we would actually be doing is moving backwards because everything around us would still be moving forward.

Have you ever been in a parked car and suddenly the car next to you starts pulling forward and in a brief moment you panic because you actually believe that you are rolling backward? I think this has happened to most of us, and even though we are sitting perfectly still, because the world around us is moving, it gives us the impression that we are actually moving backward.

Below is one of the few illustrations you will find in this book, but I feel like for this topic, it is really effective to see an actual visual of the success cycle. Feel free to show this to your son or daughter when you are teaching this to them. This can be a really effective tool.

↗ SUCCESS ↘

HABITS   CONFIDENCE

↖ ACTIVITY ↙

The direction you move in this cycle is completely dependent upon you. I will tell you, however, that if you think you are stuck and not getting anywhere, what is actually happening is that you are moving backward because there is no such thing as stuck.

Now that you have a visual of what the success cycle looks like, I am going explain how it works and how you as a coach fit into the cycle. The cycle starts with success, any success. This can be big, like winning a big game, or small, like brushing your teeth seven days in a row. It makes no difference the size of the success.

I really want you to understand this because a lot of people I work with think they are a failure because they have not reached the level they would consider success, and what this thinking does is move you backward on the success cycle even faster than standing still, but we will get more into that later in this chapter.

What is important to understand here is that any success, no matter how big or small you perceive it to be, equals the exact same number to your subconscious mind, one, a single success. Too often we think we have to have a big success in order to feel good and move through the cycle, and all you really need is any success. What is important is that you recognize that success.

Let's use an example of a baseball player. A first-year player catches the ball in the air with his/her glove for the first time ever. This is a success, and it builds their confidence and motivates them to do more activity, which in this case, would be to catch more balls. Then by catching more balls, this eventually creates a habit. This habit then creates a consistent result that is catching the ball more times than missing it. As long as the player focuses on their success—catching the ball—he or she will continue to move forward in the success cycle and get better and better.

How this relates to your child at home is that you start the cycle by recognizing their success. Let's say for instance that your child says please or thank you at the appropriate time. You would recognize them for doing the right thing at the appropriate time, and this would bring their attention to the success they just had. You would be helping them to build their confidence and they would be motivated to do this more often. As they do this more often, eventually it becomes a habit, and they do it without thinking.

Because you recognized a small success, you have helped to develop a polite young man or woman. And yes, it is that simple. Let's take another example. Let's say your child is currently failing one of his/her classes, and you start working with them and supporting them. You would not want to wait until their grades come out the next time to recognize them. You might first recognize them for spending extra time studying, and when you do this they will feel good about themselves (confidence) and they will do it again (activity) and after doing it over and over again, it will become a good (habit).

When the report card finally comes out, they will see an improved result because the success cycle always works. It works every time, and you are in complete control of this at all times. You can't start at the end result; you have to start with recognizing the smallest thing you can find that they are doing in the beginning that you know is a good thing to be doing. This starts the cycle; do this with anything they are doing in a way that gets them motivated and confident every time you recognize it, and watch what happens. You will be amazed at how well this works.

Professional athletes realize this, so let's use a great example. Let's say a hitter goes into a slump. What does he do? He changes a pattern, breaks the backward success cycle, and then he might go back to the cages and work off a tee on his fundamentals, then hit off a live pitcher while being coached through his mechanics, and eventually his results will change at the plate in the game. But it never starts there. That is the end point, the results are the last thing you see in the cycle. This is why if you start by celebrating the little things you can get the cycle going, and your children will stay motivated because they are experiencing the success cycle. If you make the success too big, then it takes too long to realize the results and your child will move backwards through the cycle because he or she is not experiencing success.

This seems like the appropriate time to talk about the reverse success cycle. What I often see, especially in young athletes, is that they define their success based on a result that is too far away from them. It is too far in the future, and they miss a lot of the progress they are making and they don't celebrate it because the results aren't there yet according to their definition of success. What then happens is every time they have an opportunity to succeed according to their definition and they don't, then they have failed. There is no in between—if you are not constantly realizing your successes, then you are constantly realizing your failures, and this starts the momentum of the success cycle in reverse.

Here is how it plays out: Your subconscious recognizes that you did not achieve what you predetermined was a success to you. When it recognizes this, it makes the assumption that you are a failure. Then you start to believe you are a failure, so you create bad habits, which then create activities that decrease your confidence. Then when your confidence goes down, you have less and less success.

Can you see how this can very quickly and easily become a real challenge for someone, especially a small child or a young athlete? A real-life example of this was when I was coaching a little league baseball team and we were losing a lot of games. In fact, that season we ended up losing every single game we played except for one that we tied. What I realized later was that all the players based their idea of success on winning the game, and anything less than that was not a success. So every time they lost a game, they moved backward in the success cycle and just spiraled down.

They started to not get along, they stopped caring about playing the games, and they stopped having fun. They began to expect to lose and so they didn't work as hard in practice, and they began to lose their motivation. They started to break out in fights among themselves, and after the season a lot of the boys went their separate ways.

This ended up being a premier example of the success cycle moving in the wrong direction, and let me tell you, when it gets momentum it is hard to stop. It's like taking the parking brake off when your car is parked at the top of a really steep hill. If you immediately change your mind and stop the car from rolling before its momentum gets going, you can stop it. If you wait till the bottom of the hill to try to stop the same car, you are not going to stop it.

I hope this has helped you to better understand the success cycle and you take this information and put it to work in your home. This will change a lot of things in your home—the confidence level, the attitudes, and the motivation of all the people in your home, to name a few.

We will talk more about setting goals and making promises that you can keep and how important that is in the next chapter. But for now, just make it a point to celebrate your successes no matter how small you may think they are, and make it a point to celebrate the successes of your child. This will be one of the best things you will ever do for him or her.

Let's do an exercise to get the success cycle started right now!

I know this may sound simple, and a little too easy, which makes it a prime candidate for skipping this exercise. Make sure you do the following exercise. It is simple, not because it does not have value, but because it is so true. Too often we perpetuate the failure cycle, or backwards movement on the success cycle, through the use of a habit. What I mean by this is that we do not even know that we are doing it. Let me give you an example of what I might do with one of my children.

1. Current Challenge: "I hate brushing my teeth"
    a. Solution:

Every time your child smiles, recognize it, make it a big deal. Go over the top with this and really lay it on them thick, (when we are doing drills on the field, we exaggerate the movements in an effort to program them into the subconscious memory, or muscle memory, we are doing the same thing here). Every time they smile, mention how great their smile is, and get them emotionally involved with this idea. Tell them how much you love it when they smile.

Now, when they are brushing their teeth, recognize it, and more importantly, connect their great smile to brushing their teeth. It might look something like this:

"Mylee, you know why you have such a fantastic smile don't you? It's because you are always taking such great care of it. I love your smile, and I swear it shines brighter every time I see you. You must be really great at brushing your teeth. I am going to start brushing my teeth better so I can have a great big smile like you some day."

Don't hold back, really make it your own and don't be afraid to pour it on! Use your own words and do what naturally comes to you, make it real for you and your child. Not only will you be building up your child's confidence, they will slowly become internally motivated to brush their teeth, and take pride in doing it well. This is only one example, so take what you know and do something that will mean something to your child, and make the small tweaks that are going to create big changes in your child. Remember, You are a Rock Star!

CHAPTER 10

Goals vs. Promises

I t has been my experience over the last twenty years that a lot more people talk about and make goals than I used to see, but unfortunately most of those people who do make those goals never keep them.

The word *goal* doesn't seem to carry the same weight that it once did. I have to think that you don't realize what you are doing when you set a goal and then break it, and what that means to you and your future success.

Let's start with the surface level. If you set a goal and you end up not being able to accomplish that goal, how do you feel? Usually you did not feel very good, and because of this you have a very clear indicator that you are starting the wrong way on the success cycle.

On the other side of the coin, when you do meet your goals you feel great, and this is an indicator that you are headed in the right direction on the success cycle. What most people don't realize is that setting a smaller interim goal actually can help you move in the right direction and keep your momentum going forward.

Every time you set a goal, you are making a new commitment to yourself, and every time you are not able to reach that goal, no matter what the reason is, you are breaking that commitment. The worst thing you can do is to ignore it, to act as if it was no big deal that you missed the goal. By not recognizing it and setting a new goal and making a new commitment you get moving the wrong way on the success cycle. Your subconscious recognizes this as a failure whether you notice it or not, and every failure moves you backwards on the success cycle until you recognize it, stop the momentum, set a new goal, and start moving forward in the success cycle again.

If you set a goal or make a commitment to yourself, keep it, and the moment you realize you can't keep the commitment, recognize it and make a new commitment. This actually stops the momentum before you get started and will save you a lot of grief in the long run. Like I said before, it is much easier to stop a parked car at the top of a hill before it starts rolling down than it is to stop it at the bottom of that same hill once it has gained momentum.

You can translate this for your kids by teaching them to set smart goals, or goals that are specific, measurable, achievable. I would recommend setting goals that are small at first, and every time they reach a goal and build up their confidence you can set a bigger goal, and then a bigger goal. Make sure you are letting the children determine their own goals. Do not set goals for your children; they are the only ones capable of knowing what they want their goals to be and what they should be. You are just there to guide them through the process.

Now let's talk about promises. Over the last year I have stopped setting goals for myself and started making promises. The reason came from an event I attended in Atlanta, Georgia. The speaker talked about goals versus promises and the difference in his mind.

I resonated with his story and maybe you will too when I share it in just a moment. He believed that the value of a "goal" has diminished and that promises were much stronger than goals. I will relate his story to you as closely as I can remember him telling it to me, and then you can make the decision for yourself on how you feel about it.

I have given a lot of thought to setting goals lately. I know how important it is to set goals, and how much more important it is to write them down, and how even more important it is to look at them every day. The challenge I have is not with setting goals, but in the value of the word goal. I feel as though a goal is not as strong a term as it once was. So I have recently made the switch to making myself promises.

For example, if you were to get married to a woman and you were at the altar stating your vows in terms of goals, it might sound like this: "I am making it my goal to be with you for the rest of my life, until death do us part, and I am making it a goal of mine to never be with another woman for that entire time."

It kind of feels like the groom is leaving a little too much room for error in the message he is sending to his bride. She may even decide that she is not willing to take a chance that he is really committed to achieving those goals as stated.

On the other hand, how does this one sound? "I promise to be with you until death do us part, and I promise to remain faithful to you for all that time." It sounds a little bit more permanent and leaves almost no room for interpretation, right? I have found that making promises to myself daily, weekly, monthly, and yearly is a much more effective way for me to achieve the level of success that I desire.

What do you think about the speaker's story? Since I converted my goals to promises, I want to give you some real examples so that you can compare my current results to my past results. Before, I would set goals with only the thought of what having achieved that goal was going to feel like to me, and I did not really consider how realistic the goal was. Then when the time frame to meet that goal came and went, it was not that big of a deal. I simply set another goal and moved on.

The moment I made my first promise to myself, I changed the promise because I immediately felt that it was unattainable and I was going to be breaking a promise to myself. I could see instantly that I was setting myself up for failure. I know where that road leads, so I reworked the equation, made a new promise, and have been keeping my promises on a consistent basis ever since.

The writing of this book is the direct result of a promise I actually made to a friend of mine. She is to thank for it being here in front of you right now. I love and respect her so much that since I made the promise to her, I am committed to keeping that promise. I realize that this is simply my state of mind and what works for me. You can call it whatever you want, that is not the important part. The important part is that whatever you call it, you keep it. Make sure you set yourself up for success.

You make the rules and this is your game you are playing, so make the rules so that you can easily win. Why not? Remember this when you are teaching it to your children. Let them make the rules and teach them that it is their game, they can make up whatever rules they want, and you would suggest they make the rules so that they always win. What will that do for your success cycle? One of my mentors always tells this story about his friend, and I feel it is appropriate to share with you here. I will share it to the best that I can recall it, and hopefully it will help illustrate my point.

I am a pretty good golfer, and I went out with my friend one time. He was always talking about how much he loved golf, too, and he wanted to go with me. So I just assumed he was a decent golfer because he did it all the time and he always enjoyed it. Most people I know who are bad golfers do not enjoy it that much.

So we get out on the course and everybody tees off, and my friend is the last to go. He shanks the shot and hits it about ten yards. Then we walk up to his ball and he hits it again, and he shanks it again and it goes about fifty yards.

After about the third hole with this going on and on, I had to ask him what his secret was, because he was laughing and joking with the rest of us just as if he was playing a great game, and what he told me after that was priceless.

He said, "A long time ago I made an agreement with myself that as long as I hit the ball forward, it was a good shot, and ever since then I have thoroughly enjoyed golfing."

I thought about his answer for a moment and then realized that I had never seen someone hit the ball backwards, so any shot he ever takes is a win for him, and therefore he always has a great time when he is golfing.

Think about that story for a moment. If you have ever golfed before, it can be an incredibly frustrating game at times, unless you make your own rules so that you win every time!

I had a client one time who was really in a bad place and no matter what I tried she just kept spiraling down, until I finally found something that worked. Here is what I said to her: "Look, I get it, your life is hard. You are the only one to ever have gone through this much stuff, and you are probably the only one ever to have had this hard of a time with this. So let's change the rules—let's call breathing a success."

She stopped crying and asked me, "What?"

I continued, "Let's mark it down in our minds and on our success chart that every time we take a breath we are experiencing success. Breathing is our new success, and then when we get really good at that, we will make a new rule and set a new success expectation."

She started to laugh and before the end of the conversation, which lasted more than two hours, she had a goal that every time she thought of her son, it was a success, and every time she got dressed it was a success, and every time she talked to a friend it was a success.

Over the next thirty days, her attitude completely changed, and although a lot of the challenges she thought were devastating and insurmountable still existed in her life, she did not feel the same way about them.

If you can get your child on the success cycle going the right direction, the size of the success makes no difference. Just get him or her moving in the right direction—that's all you have to do.

A Goal vs. A Promise
Some questions you might want to ask yourself:

1. What does the word "Goal" mean to you?
   a. Really stop to think about this for a moment before you answer.
1. What does the word "Promise" mean to you?

Now, take the one that is more powerful, or meaningful to you and use that one from this moment forward. I promise you, this will change your results, even if you choose to use the same word!

CHAPTER 11

Why Fear Is a Great Motivator

Earlier in this book, I gave you an acronym for fear; do you remember it? I hope so, but just in case you forgot it, I am going to give it to you again: False Evidence Appearing Real.

Why am I talking to you now about what a great motivator fear can be? Here is the real truth: Most people cannot just eliminate fear from their reality right away, so I had to figure out a way to use it in order to keep people going on the right track. What I found was that if you use fear as a motivator instead of a roadblock, it can propel you extremely fast in the direction of your dream.

The key is that you have to be able to *use* the fear—it cannot be the other way around because if fear is using you, it is preventing you from achieving your goals or promises. So the question remains, How can I use fear to my advantage?

The answer is in the title to this chapter, Fear Is a Great Motivator. Think about it—when we are motivated to do something, we are either motivated by what we will get from doing the activity or we are motivated by what will happen if we don't do the activity. Are you starting to see this now? Let's jump straight into a story that is a perfect example of being motivated by fear.

As a teenager, I had a brother who had three little kids—two boys and a girl. I used to babysit them for him, and I was not the most responsible of babysitters. Let's just say that I usually had my own agenda. But there was one thing we all knew very well. My sister-in-law got off work at the bank at the same time every day, and she was consistently home at the same time every day. She had pretty much only one rule, and that was that the house must be clean when she got home so that she did not have to worry about it after working hard all day long at the bank.

So my nephews, my niece, and I all had an unspoken agreement. We could play hard all day, trash the house, and at a certain moment, the games would stop, the radio would be cranked up and we would clean the heck out of that house absolutely as fast as we could, with the understanding that it was full speed ahead until it was done and always before Bea got home.

The thing you should know about my sister-in-law is that she is a very strong-willed woman from

Venezuela, and when she gets angry, the trees move to get out of her way.

Do you think that in the story above we were motivated by the house being clean, or by the fear of what would happen if the house was not clean when Bea got home?

We were so afraid of her getting home and the house not being clean, that we could clean that house in record time with amazing quality. We were definitely using fear as a great motivator.

As a parent, you have to be really careful about using fear as a motivator. The number one reason is: Do you really want your kids to be afraid of you? The second is that it never lasts. You can lead and motivate by fear for only so long, then you lose the respect of those following you, and at that point you will not be able to lead them anymore. You are of no use to your organization anymore, even if that organization is your own household.

This is a tough pill to swallow, but let's put it in a context that might make more sense. Have you ever seen a new football coach come into the NFL and have incredible success for a few years and then just appear to fall flat on his face after that? Of course you have if you follow the NFL at all. This is what has happened. The coach comes in, tries to take over and lead by fear—whatever that fear may be—and it works, but only for a short time. Fear is never a be all, end all. All dictators fall; this is the way it is.

I will not even go into what happens to a leader who leads in this way for a long period of time, but a long story short is that his or her body will begin to fail and fall apart. No amount of money can fix that.

The only time I use fear as a motivator is if I find myself in a situation where the time is running out, and there is already fear in the air. I then use the existing fear to motivate my team, but I would never make up that fear just to motivate the team. I have seen what it can do if directed in the wrong direction and how it can damage kids, so although I felt it appropriate to mention here and dedicated this chapter to this subject, I would not recommend that you make a habit of leading your family through fear. This is not part of a long-term plan and I am just going to assume that you are in it for the long hall with your family.

You will find yourself in a position from time to time where fear is the right answer and the best answer in that moment. And hopefully this chapter has helped you to define when that moment might be and what to do when you find yourself in it.

A few words of caution and guidance on when to use fear as a motivator

1.   Leverage fear to your advantage only when it already exists, do not create it.
2.   Be careful not to form the habit of using fear to motivate your kids.

3. This is a short-term solution, by it's own nature
    it cannot be a long-term solution.

Pay attention to your gut, and trust that you will
know when it is appropriate to use fear, and when it
is not. It can and will be a great motivator when used
properly.

CHAPTER 12

The Easiest Way to Miss Your Target

This chapter is dedicated to a good friend of mine who is an incredible person. I have only known him for a short time, but it took me just a few seconds to realize what a great man he is. I was interviewing him and he said something I thought was brilliant and I am going to quote him here:

> *"The easiest way to miss your target is to look away from it. I may not know exactly how to help you hit your target, but I definitely know the easiest and most sure fire way to miss it, and that is to simply take your eyes off it, even for a second."*
> ~ Master Christophe Clarke

If you get that, there is no more to be said on this subject. You will always get what you focus on, and when you look away from your goal, you cannot at the same time be focused on it. Earl Nightingale, a well-known thought leader, produced the first non-music record album that sold over a million copies—called "The Greatest Secret." Earl summed it up perfectly when he said, "The strangest secret is that a man becomes what he thinks about most of the time."

What a great way to say it! If you have a dream, you think about it, and the more you think about it the more real it becomes. If a dream remains a dream and does not come into reality, this happens because when you have the dream, you dismiss it as a dream and you don't spend any time thinking about it. I want to put this in perspective for you. Think about the last time you shot an arrow or a bullet at a target or you threw something at a target? Were you looking at the target? Of course you were unless you were fooling around because usually in order to hit the target, you have to look at it.

When I was a young man, I was in Boy Scouts and I was on a scouting trip with one of my friends. We got the opportunity to earn our rifle merit badge. The rifle we were shooting was, I believe, a twelve-gauge shotgun actually, but don't quote me on that.

The point is that when it was my friend's turn to shoot, he was afraid of the sound and the kickback that the rifle had. He was much smaller than most of the boys and because of that, he was really scared. But he was not going to be outdone by the rest of us, so he was going to take his turn with the rifle despite his fear.

When he took his first shot I looked over at him because I noticed that it looked like his gun was really aimed off target, and when I looked at him just before he fired, I noticed his eyes were closed. He missed the target big time.

I asked him why he was closing his eyes and he said it was because he was afraid. I somehow convinced him that the gun would provide the kickback and the sound whether his eyes were closed or not, and the safety goggles he was wearing were going to protect his eyes whether they were open or closed. His next shot hit the water-filled gas can (the target) dead center. This was a perfect example of the easiest way to miss your target: Take your eyes off it.

In thinking about this and writing this chapter, I suppose there is one way that is easier to miss your target than to take your eyes off it, and that would be to not have a target at all. This seems really obvious, but how many people do you know who don't have goals or dreams that they are currently working on? I would venture to say that it is probably more than you can count. Do you remember the earlier chapter when I was talking to you about your purpose? Do you have a target? If you didn't before, I hope you do now.

So how do you translate this into something your children can understand? One way would be to use examples of things that they have wanted over time and that they have gotten. A perfect example would be a Christmas or birthday gift that they really wanted and could not stop talking about or thinking about. Make sure it is one that they did end up receiving. Then talk to them about how that was their target, and because they were constantly thinking about it, talking about it, and praying for it, they got it. If they want anything in life, they can go about achieving it through this same process.

Napoleon Hill says it like this, "Define your dream, and get a burning desire for its achievement." Depending on the age of your child, you can talk to him or her about your first girlfriend or boyfriend. When you first met them, from that moment on you could not get them off your mind, and all you did was think about them day and night. This is what Napoleon Hill means by defining your dream (girlfriend/boyfriend) and then getting a magnificent obsession for its achievement (think about him or her all the time). However you do it, just make sure that your child always has a target, something he is shooting for, and what he achieves will surprise even you.

What is your target?

Take a moment and write out the answer to the proceeding question. If your answer is well defined, and can be interpreted and understood clearly by someone else, then you have a solid target. If no one but you understands what you just wrote down, it might be time to re-define your target.

Now, how do you apply this to your kid?

The easiest way is to make a game of it. So, let's do that!

What you will need:

1. A large poster board
2. Markers
3. Bean bags or some other soft flying object
4. Masking tape
5. A Blindfold
6. A Piece of notebook paper

Start by drawing a target on the poster board. Remember, bigger is better, more colors are always better than less, and be creative. Have your kids help you with this, make it fun, and they will love it!

Next, hang up the poster board and decide how far you want the throw line to be from the target. Keep in mind your child's current ability, and age, make it so they can win easily. Then mark the spot with the masking tape by taping a line to the floor. If you have multiple children of different ages and abilities, don't be afraid to have them each make their own line, and the distance that is appropriate for them. The older ones may challenge you and suggest that this is not fair, just explain to them that it is important that everyone wins in this game, and that they are not competing against each other, but instead, they are only competing with themselves.

Next, take your paper and write numbers down the left hand side. The numbers should equal the number of players in the game. Write down the name of each player next to a number. This is now the order the players will throw in. You can make up your own rules to decide who goes first, I would encourage you to stay away from the following; youngest first, oldest first, and alphabetical order. Remember, we are creating new neural pathways here, so have fun with this and most importantly, be creative!

Rounds 1,2,3. Now have each player take turns throwing at the target from behind their line. Encourage them to use whatever throwing style or form they feel most comfortable with, do not limit them here. Give each player multiple throws each round, I would suggest a minimum of three, but you can do whatever you want here. Allow them to look at the target in this first round, you will not need the blindfold yet. Next to each player's name use tally marks to keep track of how many times they hit the target. Repeat this the same way for a total of 3 rounds.

Rounds 4,5,6. Now we get to the fun part of this lesson. Start this round with the first player again. This time, blindfold the player before they throw, and then spin them three or more times before they throw at the target. Remember to leave them facing the target when you get done spinning them, even a blind man will sometimes hit his target! Make sure to keep score with your tally marks again. You are going to total the scores from the first 3 rounds for each of the players, and then do the same for the second 3 rounds.

Once everyone has completed all their rounds, total up all the scores. The results may vary some, but by now you get the picture. You will see that this seems obvious now that you have played the game, but you never know what your children will think, and how differently they will look at goals now.

The last part of the game is to sit down and discuss these results with your children, take a few minutes, maybe over some sort of prize dessert or something, and discuss their results. Remember, they will have discovered something here, so see what it is. You may need to lead the discussion, but make sure you allow them to come up with their own conclusions as to why they got the results they did. I promise you, they will suprise you with their answers.

Repeat this game as often as you want. Your children will love the friendly competition, and the lesson is valuable enough that you will want them to experience it more than once.

CHAPTER 13

Building Your Foundation

Hopefully by now you have realized that everything I have been talking to you about so far has been the basic fundamentals, or what some would call the foundation for becoming a better parent. I have written this book in the same way that I coach any athlete, any team, or any business owner. I strip what they are trying to do down to the basic fundamentals (the foundation) and I make sure that they understand those fundamentals before we move on.

One of my mentors used to always say, "You can only build as high up as your foundation is deep." What this means to me is that you have to have a strong foundation if you want to build a big building.

Have you ever heard the saying, "Your team is only as strong as your weakest link"? You probably have, and the same can be said for your building: Your building is only as strong as your foundation. If your foundation fails, then your building is going to fall. This is why to this day I only teach the basic fundamentals. There are all kinds of interesting new techniques and training tools that you can use to improve your game, and they all work when used correctly, but there are basic fundamentals that have to be mastered in order for you to succeed on the field, in life, and in business. If you can strip something down to the basics, and you can communicate those basic principles to whomever you are trying to teach, you will have more success than most.

Too many coaches or parents get caught up in the latest and greatest widget or technique that is the trend right now, and they forget about the basics. When this happens, you lose. You will lose players, respect, and games because the winning stops if you do not have the fundamentals mastered. The caveat is that you will never really have them mastered because you can always get better.

One of the most incredible examples of this is Albert Pujols. Before every game he goes into the batting cage and takes somewhere between two and three hundred swings. Now most kids don't believe me when I say that, so I tell them to Google it, and they do, and sure enough they find it. Most people would consider him to be one of the greatest hitters in baseball, but he still takes that many swings off the tee? I would say it is because he is constantly working on the fundamentals that he is one of the greatest hitters in baseball. I think it's funny when my high school athletes tell me that the tees are for little kids, and then I show them Albert Pujols and they can't believe he does that.

Then when we are taking grounders in the infield, the players occasionally tell me that they want to work on the hard ground balls and the diving plays just like the pros do. I ask them how many times they have seen a professional baseball player practicing diving after a ball. The answer is usually never, and rightfully so. Professional players do not work on the incredible, spectacular plays in practice; they work on the fundamentals. And the more they master those fundamentals, the more spectacular plays they make in the game.

Jerry Rice was one of the hardest-working receivers of all time. It is no coincidence that he is also one of the most highly decorated receivers of all time. If you study Jerry at all, you will quickly figure out that his workouts were nothing special. Sure, they were hard and focused, but they were focused on the basic moves and fundamentals of receiving the football. And no one would argue that Jerry made more than his fair share of spectacular plays in games all throughout his storied NFL career.

So how do you relate this all to your child? Easy, break it down for her, teach her the things that I have outlined for you in this book. As you learn it better, teach it to her and never stray far from the basics, because you don't ever have to. In fact, you want to study these basics until you know them better than you know the back of your hand. Better than you know your own name.

What will this do for you and your child? Everything. This will change the way you think, which will in turn change the way you act, which will in turn change the habits you have, and with new habits come new results on auto pilot. Yes, you are a rock star, and everything you will ever need, you already have.

I am just making you a little more aware of your greatness. That's what it's all about, right? You becoming more aware of how great you really are. Just share your greatness with your children, and they will never need any more than that from you. And you will never be able to give them anything greater than that!

Something to consider before moving on to the next chapter

How do you teach a child the importance of mastering the fundamentals, and more importantly, how do you keep them engaged in the same activity over and over again? I like to tell them to watch the movie "Karate Kid", but I understand that movie is getting a little old, and a lot of our children have never seen it. So I will give you a different way.

The easiest exercise I have ever used is as follows:

Take building blocks of any kind, Legos usually work the best, but you just need something that is stackable. Set up two building zones, separate your children into two teams, and then give the first set of instructions to the first team, and the second set of instructions to the other team.

The object of this game is to build the tallest tower you can. Whoever builds it the highest wins. The one rule is that the winning tower must withstand a little wind. This could be you blowing on the tower, or turning on a fan. If the tallest tower falls when the wind is applied to it, then the one left standing is the winner. Remember, the winner is the tallest tower still standing.

Zone 1 instructions: The builder cannot stack bricks side by side at all, he/she can only stack one on top of another, and go as high as he/she can. Remember, the object is to build the tallest tower.

Zone 2 instructions: The builder must build four blocks square as the minimum base, before they can add the second level. Remember, the object is to build the tallest tower.

Now, use your fan, or huff and puff and attempt to blow down each tower, if one tower falls and the other stands, then the one left standing wins. You can make the game more exciting by adding a time element if you want, or have your kids make up some additional rules on timing to get them more engaged.

After you finish the game, ask your kids why they think the winner was successful? Why was it that their tower was able to withstand adversity? How important was it to have a bigger foundation to their tower? Why do they think that building with the wider base made for a stronger tower?

Now, relate the game to the information in this chapter. This will be a valuable lesson for everyone involved.

CHAPTER 14

Decision

———

What is a decision? What does it mean to you? Why is this important? A decision can be defined as looking at what you don't want, turning your back to it, and then looking at what you do want and making the following powerful statement: "I am going to do it; that's it, period!".

When you define a decision like this, you quickly start to see how important it is to make a decision. How do you know where you are going or even what you want if you do not make a decision? The answer is simple: You don't.

Would you believe that the majority of people on this planet are moving through their lives on autopilot, having no idea what they want? Seems really silly to you, right? Well, it's true, unfortunately. The majority of people believe that if they don't make a decision, they will not get hurt. I can tell you that this could not be further from the truth.

Making no decision can often be the worst decision you could possibly make. Yet this is a trap I see clients and friends fall into all the time. This is not unusual. A perfect example can be seen in a real estate company I own. I see new deals on my desk almost every day, and I look at them, pick out the best deals, and send them to our investors to take a look at.

There are two types of investors on my list: those who make decisions and those who don't. Another way to say it is that those who make money with their money and those who watch opportunity after opportunity pass them by because they are waiting for the golden deal or the absolutely perfect investment that meets all their criteria in all areas.

A friend said recently that there is no perfect investment ever, so you get as close as you can to perfect and you take that one. I was at a seminar earlier this year and the speaker said something that really stuck with me. He said, "The acronym for POOR people is as follows: Passes Over Opportunity Regularly." I thought that was brilliantly put, and it is so true. I see it every day.

One of my companies consults businesses on how to find hidden capital they already have and don't realize. If you had an extra twenty, thirty, or forty thousand dollars, what would you do with it? Would you continue to pass over opportunities regularly, or would you make a different decision and take advantage of the opportunities that already exist in front of you right now?

Science has discovered that you take in approximately twenty-two million bits of information every second through all of your different sensory organs. You are only consciously aware of about one hundred and sixty-four of those bits of information. So the question becomes, which bits of information are you consciously choosing to accept? You were blessed with the ability to choose which bits of information you accept and consciously recognize. This is why two people could witness the exact same accident, at the exact same time, and tell two completely different stories as to what happened. Both are telling the truth from their viewpoint, and both are telling exactly what they remember seeing; the difference is that one has different filters from the other.

The same is true when two people are sitting right next to each other and one describes an event as the most life-changing and riveting event they have ever attended and the other says they want their money back. All I want to do is to get you to realize that you are the one choosing what it is that you see and remember. So why not choose to see the bright side or the good side of everything? Both sides exist at the same time, but you can only look at one side of the coin at a time.

How do I relate this to my son or daughter? The short answer is make sure you are cultivating a positive attitude and that will train them naturally to find the gold in every situation. You want to simply guide their focus to where it started with all of us when we were born. We saw the world in all its wonders, and we were amazed, and then over time we somehow lost that sense of wonder, and we became skeptical.

If you can cultivate the wonder and bring it back to the surface and re-instill that sense of amazement at the beauty and life that surrounds us every day, you will equip your children with the information and tools they need to make decisions. Leaders always possess the ability to make decisions on the fly. They prepare their minds in advance of the decision in anticipation of having to make a decision on the fly, and then when the time comes to make a decision, they do so with complete confidence and resolve.

I am making the assumption that you are a leader, and that is why you are reading this book right now. That is why you have made it this far. You possess the qualities of a leader, and all you need to do is be you, and you will pass those qualities on to your son or daughter. Remember, it is not what you say that makes a difference in their lives, it is what you do. The fact that you have made the decision to finish this book is setting an example of follow through and commitment that you probably did not even consider when you made that decision.

The further you dive into the basics of anything, the closer to the truth you come, and the simpler it is. Don't make it harder than it has to be. You are a great parent or you would not be reading this book. What I have realized over time is that if you possess the ability to make quick decisions, you most likely also possess the ability to make complicated things simple. So put what I am giving you into your own words and your own actions and then give it to your children naturally.

You can do it, I know you can.

How to teach this lesson to your children

First, make the decision that this is something that you really want to teach your children. Then play the following game with them:

What you will need:
1. 2 pieces of poster board
2. Markers
3. A prize for the winner/s
4. Dice

First, divide your household into two teams. Then give markers and a sheet of paper to each team. Give each team the following instructions separately being careful that the teams do not hear each other's instructions.

Team 1 instructions:

1. You must draw a map to the garage from a room in your house. (this could be any room in your house, ideally the one farthest away from the garage)

2. You must design obstacles, steps and or spaces on your game board that have instructions on them. Be creative, and make sure some of the spaces move you forward and or skip steps, and others send you backward. Make sure to include spaces that might move you all the way back to the start, or skip you all the way to the finish.

3. You must have a minimum of 20 steps/spaces on your board.

4. Have fun, this is a game, make sure to be creative in this process. The more creative you are, the more fun the game will be.

Team 2 instructions:

1. Same as the instructions in step one for Team 1.

2. You must design obstacles and steps where the player has to choose option 1 or option 2. Every single space will need to have 2 options. It is always the players decision which instructions they want to follow. Make sure that one of the choices moves the player backwards on the board, and the other moves them forward.

3. You must have a minimum of 20 steps/spaces on your board.

4. Have fun with this. Remember to make sure that each space has one option that will move the player forward, and one option that will move them backward on the board.

5. For added fun, you can make some of the spaces a must stop, meaning each player has to stop on that space and do something to collect the key to the garage door or something like that.

Now, have each individual roll the dice, whoever rolls the highest number will go first. Then play will move clockwise around the board. First play the game with Team 1's board, where all the decisions are made for you, and your success is determined by your luck. Make sure to join in the fun, this is an incredible game. Then play Team 2's board. Keep track of how many moves it takes each player on each board to get to the garage. Now give out your prize for all who played, and while you are enjoying it, discuss what they learned from the two different boards. Remember, you want to simply lead the discussion, whatever they learned is perfect. Here are some examples of talking points to help guide your discussion.

1. Even though the one board made all the decisions for us, did we get to our goal faster?

2. I like to make my own choices, because I trust that I will always make the best decision for me.

3. I always make decisions that move me toward my goal. As long as I know what my goal is, I naturally move towards it.

The final lesson in this chapter is that no decision is bad. Some decisions slow you down, and some speed you up, but notice that you always end up where you want to go. In other words, don't put so much pressure on yourself about making "the right" decision. Just make a decision and move. You will always get where you want to go. And remember, the best person at making decisions for you, will always be you.

Now, if you want to add one more twist, just to see how this works, have someone else make the decisions for you, and you make the decisions for them. Do this on board 2, and remember the object is for YOU to get to your goal first, and not the person you are making the decisions for. You will notice that any time we are making decisions, it is always from our point of view, with our best interests in mind, and can never be anything different, no matter what we think. We are naturally moving toward our own goals.

CHAPTER 15

What Are You Grateful For?

I am going to use this section to stress the importance of realizing how blessed you really are. Just the fact that you have a copy of this book in your hands means that you are blessed more than most of the people on this planet. Not because this is such a great book, but because it is a book, and there are more people who do not have access to this than do. So you are in the minority. Given the fact that you are reading this book, it is most likely that you are a parent or someone who loves kids, and you want to know how to make a difference in their lives. So I am grateful for you.

My mission is to empower kids to achieve in life, and if I can do part of that through you, then you are helping me to fulfill my mission. Hopefully you will take something from this book that will help you fulfill your purpose and then I will know that it was worth it for me to sit here and write this book. I put on a seminar once with a group of life coaches who, in their own right, were all successful and powerful human beings, and when we were all in the same room with the same intentions, it was one of the most powerful things I ever witnessed. I saw those who were in attendance change while they were in the room. I felt that even though it was a small group, everyone who was there got more than they paid for, including me.

The title of the seminar was "The Formula for Success = Gratitude + Goals + Persistence." I mention this because when you start from a state of gratitude, everything you see appears to be better. The day is better; your relationship is better; the colors in your home are brighter; and you radiate a sense of love and caring that no one can put a value on.

One of the most powerful things I do almost every day is to go through in my head a list of the things I am grateful for in that moment. There was a time in my life when I went through a state of depression, and the only thing I could find to be grateful for was my ability to be alive and with my kids because at the time I was out of work. And now, there is more to be thankful for than I can list in any one day. If I were to start the list in the morning, I could not complete it by night fall.

If you can be in a constant state of gratitude, you will accomplish magnificent things, and most importantly, your children will notice. Your friends will be influenced by your ever-positive glow, and your relationships will be strengthened. Gratitude never hurt anyone, and it always makes everyone and everything better. There are no exceptions. When was the last time you took the time to sit down and list all the things you are grateful for? If you are like most people reading this right now, I would guess that it has been a while. Even if you do this regularly, do you do it with your children? Do you make it a point to tell them every day just how truly grateful for them you are?

There is no one alive on this planet who cannot find one thing they are grateful for, and if you live in the United States of America, you have a lot to be grateful for. I recently attended a charity softball game in Colorado Springs, Colorado, in which it was celebrities against military veterans. It was one of the most amazing experiences of my life. I saw soldiers with missing limbs, burned and badly scarred bodies who had more gratitude in their pinky finger than I have personally expressed in my entire life. If you are ever in a situation where you are feeling like you have nothing you can be grateful for, I would encourage you to visit a veterans' home, or go to a charity event where you can see these men and women in action. It is the most amazing and spectacular thing I have ever seen.

When you are in their presence, you can feel their overwhelming gratitude that they are still here and that they often have a story to tell that they know will change the lives of those they share it with. They have a renewed sense of purpose, knowing that what happened to them happened for a reason, and that if they sat at home in self-pity, they would not be taking responsibility for the powerful story they have been blessed with. Yes, you heard me right. They were blessed with the gift of a powerful story, and they are sharing it with everyone who will listen.

What is your story? Who are you sharing it with? I hope with all my heart that at the very least you are sharing it with your family. They deserve as much as anyone to know your story. You may think you don't have a story or that no one wants to hear your story, but you would be wrong. What if there was one person who was on the brink of suicide and he/she heard your story and that stopped them and was the catalyst that turned their life around? Would you think your story was important and powerful then?

I know I have said this before, and I will repeat it here. You are special and unique, and no matter what anyone tells you or what you tell yourself, you have a story. And when you share your story with friends, with family, or with the world, you are making a difference. Your story is meant to be told, and I don't know your story. But I pray to God every day that I will one day know it, and the only way that prayer will come true is if you share it. So I am going to thank you in advance for sharing your story with me and with your kids. What you do by sharing your story with them, you cannot put a price on. Your story is what makes you, you, and nothing can be more exciting and exhilarating than that. I am sorry that I have gotten a little off topic here, but at the same time I want you to know that I am grateful for you and for your story, and for the impact you will have on those around you by sharing your story. This is how change happens, and it all starts with you.

What are you grateful for?

It's time to make a list of what you are grateful for. Take the next twenty minutes and write down everything you are grateful for, and make sure to include everyone that you are grateful for too! On a separate sheet of paper, write the numbers 1-10 on the left hand side. Every time you see someone's name that you wrote down on your gratitude list, write it down in order next to each number. Once you have ten names on your list, you can stop.

Ok, when was the last time you told any of these people how grateful you are that they are a part of your life? When was the last time you truly gave thanks for what they have done for you? Make it a point to reach out to your top ten and tell them how grateful you are for them. You will make their day, always, and you will notice a change in you at the same time. After you have completed this exercise, and contacted your top ten, ask yourself the following questions:

1. What are you grateful for now?

How will you show your gratitude from this day forward?

CHAPTER 16

What Makes This All Work?

————

S ince we are nearing the end of our journey together in the context of this book, I thought I would insert this chapter on what makes this whole thing work right here. I know we have gone over a lot together in the pages of this book, and I have given you a lot to think about in your life and with your parenting of the most amazing children on the planet.

What I want to talk about now is in fact what drives all this, what makes this all tic. Hopefully by now I have relayed to you my belief in what I have printed on these pages for you. My intention was, as it is every time I walk onto a baseball field as a coach, to allow you to borrow my belief in what I am teaching you until you have time to discover, test, and develop your own beliefs about this information. I pray that as you read this, you can feel my love for you and your family and the admiration I have for you. It is my intention to share my story and what I know to be true, and for you to take from my story only what you need and discard the rest.

Behind these words is what makes this all work. My powerful beliefs and positive intentions are what makes me a successful coach at home, on the field, and in business. It is nothing more or less than that. I have complete faith that what I am giving you is the truth as I know it. I have practiced these things I have taught you for years, and every day I receive new and compelling evidence that what I am talking about is true. Every single day my life gets better and better, and that is what I wish for you too. I want you to have what I have. I want you to share what I know because I have seen it impact the lives of hundreds of kids, and I know that with your help, I will be able to impact the lives of many more.

The only thing I ask is that you give the principles in this book thirty days, not months or years or decades, just one month. I promise you here and now that if you commit to practicing just one of the tools I have given you in this book for thirty days, at the end of that time you will look back on when you started and you will not recognize the man or woman you were compared to who you will be at the end of thirty days. I believe this with all of my heart and soul and I know that you can feel that coming through this book now.

Even if you never take action on one thing in this book, you are different now than you were when you started reading it. I have left a mark on this book that changes everyone it comes in contact with. There are some things here that cannot be un-seen, and they cannot be un-learned. You are a better person for having made it this far. I know this.

The last thing that makes all of this come together and work for you is persistence. We live in this modern world where everything is at our fingertips in a second, and we have access to the greatest minds on the planet in milliseconds through the miracle we call Google and the internet. We live in such an instant gratification world that people who show persistence in anything are few and far between. But this is one of the key ingredients that you find in all those who have come before you who have experienced any kind of long-term success. They all persisted through more trials than you can even imagine, and they kept going because they were committed to living their lives on purpose.

I live by a great saying I first heard from author and speaker Lisa Nichols: "Winners never quit, and quitters never win." If you really think about this and dissect it, it is so true. Because if you're winning you don't quit, and if you never quit, eventually you win.

Think about that for a moment. If you were to study every person who experienced what we call success in this world, you would find that they had the quality of persistence because this is one of the essential qualities and building blocks of success. You will find this in almost any success book that you read that has any merit. Almost any seminar worth its cost will include this principle. If you could pass on only one thing in this lifetime to your children, this would be it. You would ensure their success in any endeavor they were to take on. It's like the Energizer Bunny—if you just keep going you will always reach your goal, and you will always outlast your competition. This value is probably one of the most unappreciated characteristic of success.

Let's think about it. It's not pretty, it's not exciting, and it's not usually that much fun, but it is in every successful human who has ever walked this planet.

I have probably failed more times than you have tried at this point in your life, and my family asks me all the time, why don't you give up and move on. And at the risk of sounding like I'm using a cliché, I have a dream. And I will not stop until I have realized that dream. I would suggest that you do the same, and if you never quit you will win.

General Patton was famous for the following statement that he made in a lot of his speeches when he was talking to his men, and this is what he said: "I will always win, because I will never lose." I would suggest that you adopt this same sort of motto in your life. I might even change it a little for you here: "I will be the best parent on this planet because I will never quit until I am."

A little something to think about for review

One of the most powerful reasons why 95% of the people who write down their goals, actually achieve them, is that when your write down your goal, you are sending out a powerful intention. If you really want something, you say so. If you really need something, you write it down and make it so.

"Nothing in this life happens without intention. That is where life starts." ~Jim Carey

CHAPTER 17

There Is a Champion in You

———

Will Rogers is famous for saying, "I never met a man I didn't like." That was a choice he made and because he made that choice, he always found the good in everyone he met. I didn't know him personally, but I imagine that he was a guy I would have loved to be around. I imagine he had a lot of friends.

What I have found is that I have never met a man or woman who did not have a champion in them. The same goes for you. There is greatness in you. I can see it, and you can feel it. This is one of the reasons you have this book in your hands right now. You have a greatness in you that is burning to come out. You know there is something more you are meant to do, and yet you have not done it yet. I don't know exactly what it is, but you do, and through the processes I have shared throughout this book, I hope that you have an even greater sense of your ability and your super powers.

I can feel the champion in you rising; he/she is stirring and we have awakened your inner champion. Look out world, here you come. King Kong ain't got nothin on you! In the words of Shawn Mendez, "Superman ain't got nothin on you." I realize that not everyone I coach is going to become a professional athlete, and that is not everyone's dream. But I also realize that everyone I coach is going to one day be a professional at something, and my promise is to allow them to be the best professional they can be, no matter what that is. Some will be professional teachers, some will be professional singers, some will be professional police officers, and it does not matter what you are. That's just perfect! You are the missing puzzle piece; you are the "Special One" everyone was looking for in the Lego movie. What you have, no one else does. What you bring to the table, no one else can bring to the table. If you don't share what you have, no one else will do it because no one else *can* do it. It's up to you!

Words of wisdom from a powerful teacher

"To be great you don't have to do great things, you just have to do little things in a great way"
~Wallace D Wattles

Remember, No one ever scored the winning goal sitting on the sideline. Take massive and immediate action, and do it now! You have no idea what tomorrow is going to bring.

Morgan James
Speakers Group

↗ www.TheMorganJamesSpeakersGroup.com

We connect Morgan James published
authors with live and online events
and audiences who will benefit
from their expertise.